To Benjamin and Abigail,
Thank you for reminding me each day that
God always keeps his promises.

C.L.

To Mum and Dad,
who so beautifully mirror the love of God
and shaped a home full of creativity and faith.

J.D.

God's Big Promises Storybook Bible | © The Good Book Company 2023. Reprinted 2023, 2024.

thegoodbook.com | thegoodbook.co.uk | thegoodbook.com.au | thegoodbook.co.nz | thegoodbook.co.in

All rights reserved. Except as may be permitted by the Copyright Act, no part of this publication may be reproduced in any form or by any means without prior permission from the publisher.

Carl Laferton has asserted his right under the Copyright, Designs and Patents Act 1988
to be identified as author of this work.

Jennifer Davison has asserted her right under the Copyright, Designs and Patents Act 1988
to be identified as illustrator of this work

Illustrations by Jennifer Davison | Design and Art Direction by André Parker

ISBN: 9781784988128 | JOB-007771 | Printed in India

GOD'S BIG PROMISES

Bible Storybook

Written by
Carl Laferton

Illustrated by
Jennifer Davison

CONTENTS

The Old Testament

1. In the Beginning	16
2. In the Garden	21
3. The Snake and the Tree	25
4. Out of the Garden	29
5. Noah Builds an Ark	33
6. The First Rainbow	39
7. The Tall Tower	42
8. God's Promises to Abram	46
9. Stars in the Sky	50
10. A Baby at Last	53
11. Jacob's Sneaky Trick	58
12. Jacob's Special Dream	63
13. Joseph in Trouble	67
14. Joseph and the King of Egypt	72
15. Joseph Meets His Brothers	77
16. A Baby in the River	81
17. Moses and the Burning Bush	85
18. Let My People Go!	89

19. The Rescue from Egypt	94
20. A Path through the Sea	98
21. God's Commands	103
22. God's Tent	107
23. Making a Not-God	111
24. Joshua, Caleb, and the Explorers	115
25. Moses Sees the Land	119
26. Rahab and the Explorers	122
27. The Walls of Jericho	126
28. Joshua Says Goodbye	131
29. Deborah, Barak, and the Big Battle	134
30. Samson Saves the Israelites	138
31. Ruth Finds a Family	143
32. Hannah's Special Son	148
33. We Want a King!	153
34. God Chooses a King	157
35. David and Goliath	161
36. A King Forever	167
37. King Solomon	171
38. Things Go Very Wrong	175
39. Elijah and the Fire	179
40. A King Is Coming	184

41. Jonah and the Big Fish	188
42. Out of the Land	196
43. Daniel in the Lions' Den	200
44. Esther the Brave Queen	207
45. Back in the Land Again	211

The New Testament

46. An Angel Visits Mary	217
47. The Angel Speaks to Joseph	220
48. Mary's Thank-You Song	224
49. Jesus Is Born	227
50. Simeon and Anna Meet Jesus	233
51. Wise Men Arrive	236
52. Jesus Escapes	239
53. The Baptism of Jesus	243
54. Jesus in the Desert	247
55. Jesus Chooses His Friends	251
56. Get Up!	255
57. A Dead Man Lives	260
58. John the Baptist's Question	264
59. Jesus and the Storm	268
60. Come Out of Him!	273

61. Jesus Raises a Dead Girl to Life	277
62. Buried Treasure	282
63. Jesus Feeds the Crowds	285
64. Who Do You Say I Am?	289
65. Jesus on the Mountain	293
66. The Good Samaritan	297
67. Jesus Teaches His Friends to Pray	302
68. The Good Shepherd	305
69. The Life after This One	309
70. The Religious Leader and the Tax Collector	313
71. Jesus and the Little Children	317
72. Zacchaeus Welcomes Jesus	321
73. The King on the Donkey	326
74. Jesus at the Temple	330
75. A New Special Meal	334
76. Praying in a Garden	338
77. The King and the Thief	341
78. Jesus Is Alive!	346
79. The Strange Stranger	350
80. Thomas Changes His Mind	354
81. Jesus Goes to Heaven	358

82. The Holy Spirit Arrives	361
83. The First Church	365
84. Philip and the Ethiopian	368
85. The Road to Damascus	373
86. The One Who Keeps God's Promises	377
87. Jesus' Friends in Philippi	381
88. Paul in Jerusalem and Rome	386
89. Paul's Letters	391
90. More Letters	396
91. What Heaven Is Like	400
92. I Am Coming Soon	404

BIG PROMISES

The Bible is a big book! There are lots and lots and **LOTS** of stories in it, and all of them are true! But the Bible is also **ONE BIG TRUE STORY.** It is the story of how God made and kept **AMAZING** promises. Keep a look out for these clues on the pages and spot God making and keeping all his promises!

	God **MAKES** a promise	God **KEEPS** a promise
To **RESCUE**		
About his **PEOPLE**		
About a good **LAND** to live in		
That he will bring **JOY** – happiness		
About a **KING**		

PROMISE PATHS

If you'd like to enjoy how God made and kept one particular type of promise, follow the paths by turning to each numbered story listed in the promise paths below... keep an eye out for the clue in most (but not all) of the stories!

The **RESCUE** path

2–3–4–5–6–8–9–16–17–19–20–30–35–40–42–45–

47–49–58–64–68–75–77–78–79–84–87–91–92

The **PEOPLE** path

2–8–9–10–11–12–13–14–15–19–21–28–40–45–49–

55–58–75–77–78–79–80–81–82–83–87–88–89–91–92

The **LAND** path

2–8–9–11–12–13–14–15–17–19–21–24–25–26–28–

40–42–45–49–58–62–75–77–78–79–81–86–91–92

The **JOY** path

2–3–5–6–8–11–12–28–40–42–45–46–48–49–50–57–

58–64–71–75–77–78–79–80–81–82–85–86–91–92

The **KING** path

8–9–10–33–34–35–36–37–38–40–42–45–46–49–51–

58–62–64–65–73–75–77–78–79–81–82–84–87–91–92

The **ONE BIG STORY IN 20 STORIES** path

1–3–4–8–17–19–21–28–36–40–49–61–64–77–78–81–82–83–91–92

1. In the Beginning
Genesis 1

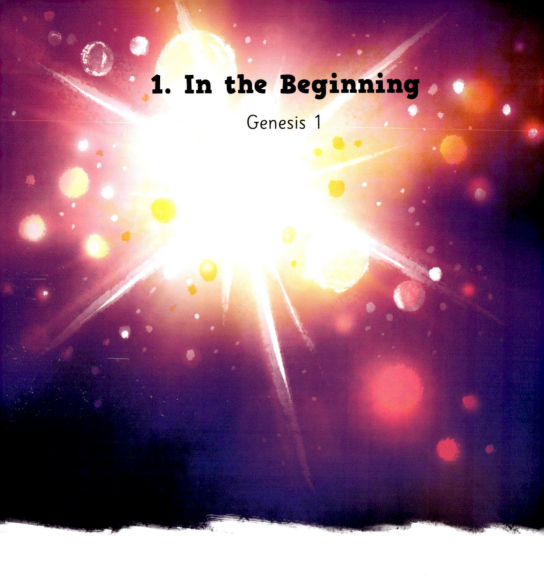

In the beginning, before there was anything else, there was God.

Then, from nothing, God made everything.

God spoke... and there was light.

God spoke... and there was sky and land and sea and plants and sun and moon.

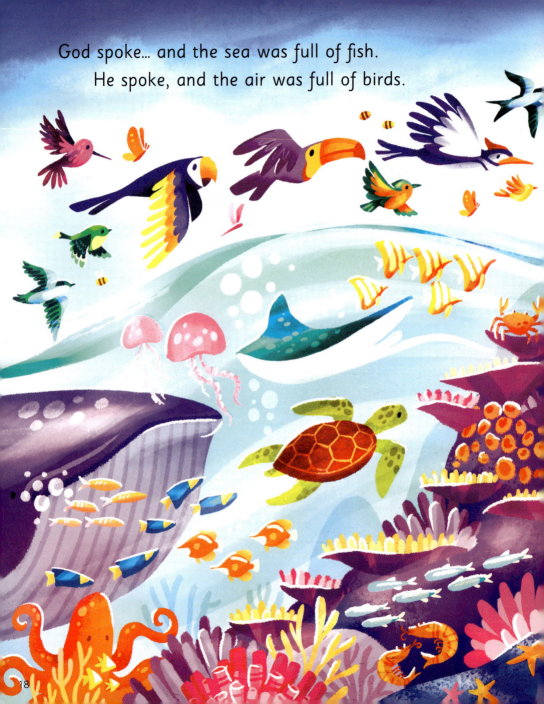

He spoke, and the land was full of all kinds of amazing animals.

Everything that God had made was good.

And then he made the best thing of all.

God made a man and a woman, called Adam and Eve. They could talk with God and be friends with God. God gave them a job: to start a family that would fill the world and to take care of the world under his good rule.

God looked at everything he had made, and it was all very good.

2. In the Garden

Genesis 2

When God made Adam, he gave him a wonderful garden to enjoy living in and taking care of. It was full of beautiful trees that were full of tasty fruit.

In the middle of the garden were two special trees.

People could eat from Special Tree Number One if they wanted to stay alive. Anyone could eat from it every day, and never die.

People could eat from Special Tree Number Two if they wanted to be in charge. Anyone could eat from it to show that they thought they should make the rules.

God gave Adam two promises. The first was "You are free to eat from any tree, including Special Tree Number One. Then you will enjoy life forever."

The second was "You must not eat from Special Tree Number Two, because you are not in charge. If you do, you won't be able to enjoy my garden forever. Instead, you will die."

God's garden was a wonderful place to live in. There was just one problem. Adam was alone. He needed someone like him to help him.

So God made a woman, Eve. Adam was really, really happy to meet her! Life in God's garden together was perfect.

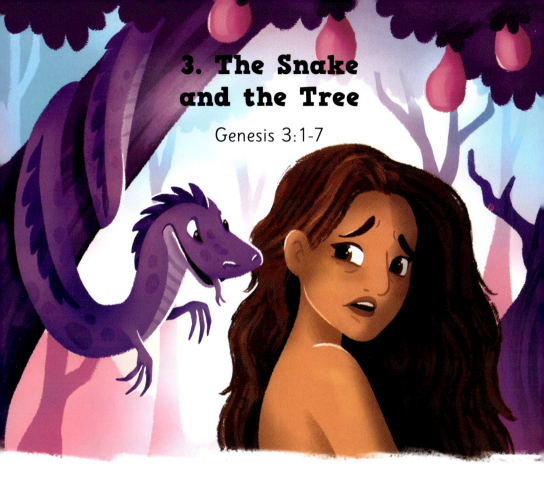

3. The Snake and the Tree

Genesis 3:1-7

There was a crafty snake in God's garden. He did not like God and he did not want to live under God's good rule.

The crafty snake asked Eve a crafty question: "Did God *really* say you must not eat from the trees in this garden?"

"No, there is only one tree that God told us not to eat from," answered Eve. "He promised that if we eat fruit from that one tree, we will die."

"You won't die if you eat from that tree!" said the snake. "No — you will be like God. You will be in charge! You will be able to make your own rules."

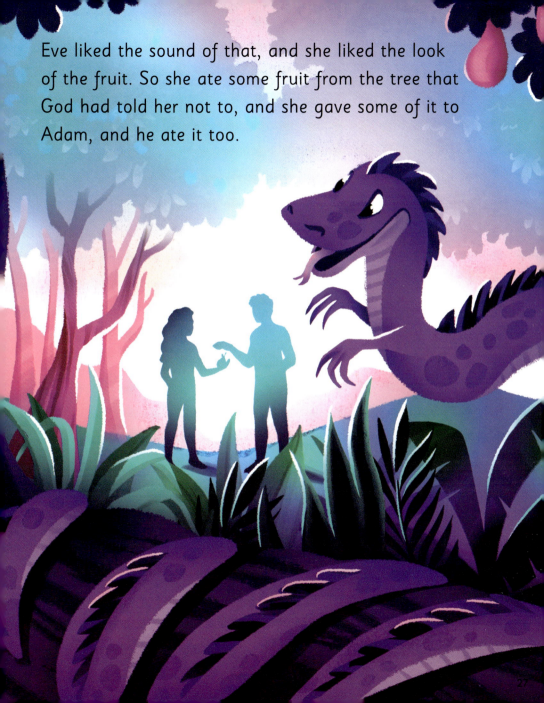

Eve liked the sound of that, and she liked the look of the fruit. So she ate some fruit from the tree that God had told her not to, and she gave some of it to Adam, and he ate it too.

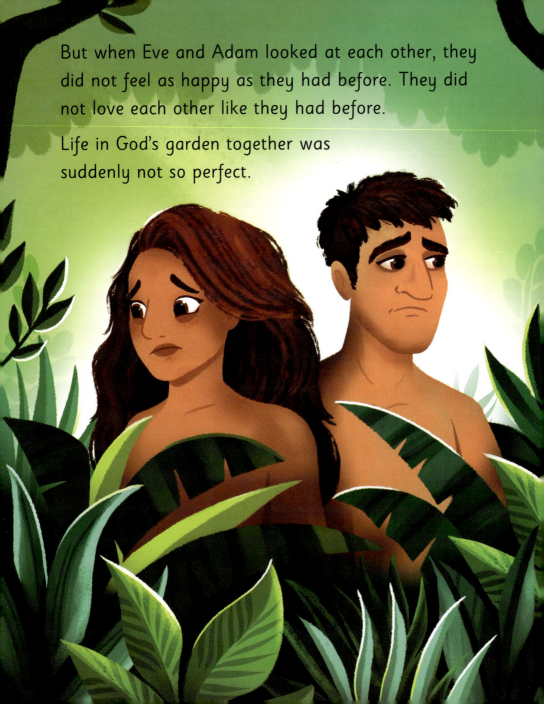

But when Eve and Adam looked at each other, they did not feel as happy as they had before. They did not love each other like they had before.

Life in God's garden together was suddenly not so perfect.

4. Out of the Garden

Genesis 3:8-24

God came to his garden to find Adam and Eve.

They knew they had eaten from the tree he had told them not to. They knew God had promised that if they did that, they would die. They felt scared, so they hid.

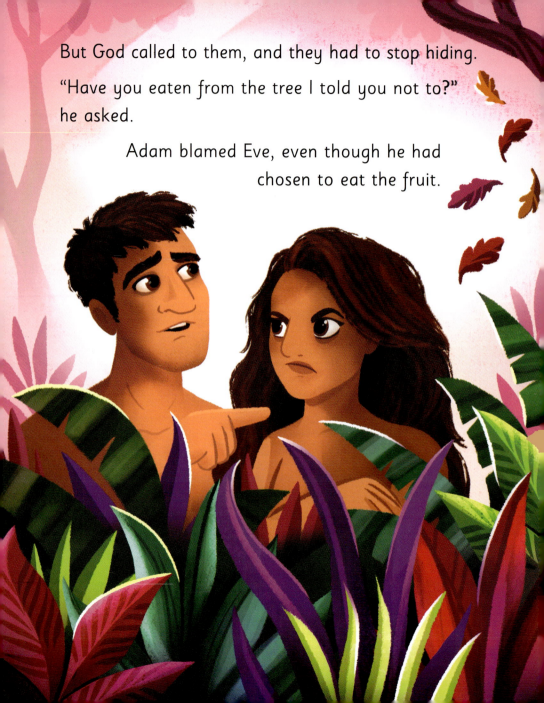

But God called to them, and they had to stop hiding.

"Have you eaten from the tree I told you not to?" he asked.

Adam blamed Eve, even though he had chosen to eat the fruit.

Eve blamed the snake, even though she had chosen to eat the fruit.

God kept his promise. He told Eve and Adam that growing a family and growing food would now be hard and painful. Even worse, they would not be able to enjoy life with God in his garden forever. One day, they would die.

But God also made another huge promise. One day, someone from Eve's family would get rid of the snake and put everything right again.

God sent Adam and Eve out of the garden. Angels with a flashing sword guarded it. No one would be able to enjoy living there with God – until his huge promise came true.

5. Noah Builds an Ark

Genesis 6:1 – 7:23

After Adam and Eve left God's wonderful garden, they had children. Those children grew up and had children, and those children grew up and had children, and they began to fill the world.

But life outside God's garden was not happy. People did not love each other. People did not love God. And people did not live forever.

God saw that people did not want to live with him in charge, and he felt sad that he had made them.

Noah was different. He loved God and wanted to live under his rule. God made him a promise:

"I am going to start again. I will send a flood that will cover the earth. So build a huge boat and take your family and some of every animal inside. I will keep you safe from the flood."

Noah believed God's promise and so he did as God said. He built a huge boat, just as God had told him to. He put some of every animal in it, and then he and his family climbed in.

Then the rain began to fall. And fall. And fall. It fell for forty days and forty nights. It covered everything: all the land... all the animals... all the people. Noah's boat was the only thing left.

But in the boat, Noah and his family and the animals with them were dry, and alive, and safe.

6. The First Rainbow

Genesis 7:24 – 9:17

When God flooded the world, everything stayed underwater for months, and months, and months.

But God had not forgotten his promise to Noah to keep him safe. So God made the waters go down until Noah's huge boat stopped floating and came to rest on dry land.

Noah and his family had been in their boat for over a year. At last, God told them to come out. All the animals came out too.

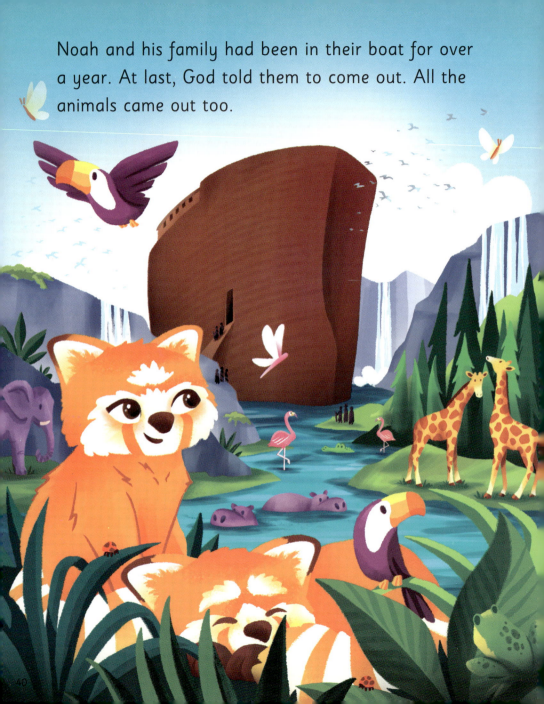

God made a promise to Noah and his family:

"I will never destroy the world in this way again. Now, fill the world with your family and take care of it."

To remind people of his promises, God put a rainbow in the sky. Whenever anyone saw a rainbow, they could remember what God had promised.

7. The Tall Tower

Genesis 11:1-9

There were more and more people, and they all spoke the same language. God had told them to fill the whole world, but they decided not to do that. Instead, they planned to build one big city and live there.

So they built lots of houses, and they started building a huge tower. "We will be famous!" they said to each other. "People will be amazed at the great things we can do!"

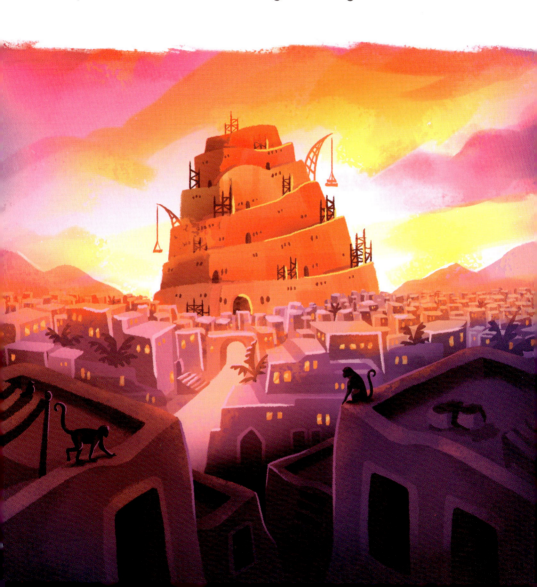

God saw the city and the tower. He wanted the people to fill the world, instead of working together to disobey him. So God caused them to stop speaking one language. Suddenly, they all spoke different languages and could not understand each other.

Now, they could not work together on their tower or their city. So the people moved to live in different places. God had made sure that people would start to fill the world — just as he'd planned.

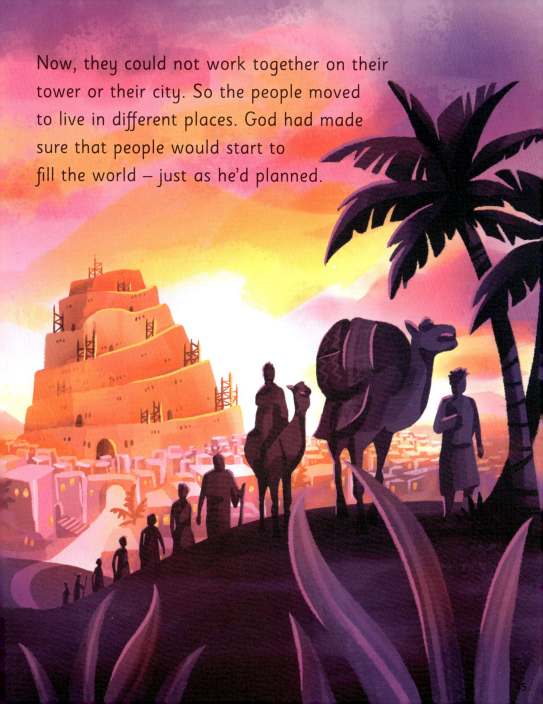

8. God's Promises to Abram

Genesis 12:1-7

A couple called Abram and Sarai lived in a land called Ur. They were SO OLD that most people their age were already grandparents — but Abram and Sarai were not even parents. They were not able to have any children to help fill the world and care for it.

One day, God told Abram,
"Leave your home and the people you know.
Go to live in the land I will show you."

Then God made a promise to Abram:

"I will give you a huge family.
I will amaze people with the great things
I do for you. I will look after you."

"I will bless you – you will live under my rule and be happy in my world.

"And I will use your family to bless people who live all over the world."

Abram believed God's promise and so he did as God said. He left his home, just as God had told him to.

When Abram and Sarai arrived in a land called Canaan, God made another promise:

"I will give this land to your family. They will live here."

9. Stars in the Sky

Genesis 15:1-21

Abram and Sarai lived in Canaan. They were now very old – and they still had no children.

Abram said to God, "You promised me a huge family that will live in this land. But how can your promise come true when I have no children? It is impossible."

"Go outside," God replied. "Look up. Try to count the stars. There are too many to count, aren't there?"

Then God made Abram another promise:

"Your family will become SO BIG that it will be as hard to count as the stars in the sky."

Abram believed God's impossible promise.
So God called Abram his friend.

That night, God appeared as a blazing fire. This was his way of making an unbreakable promise to Abram:

"You will have a huge family," God said. "For a long time, they will live somewhere else. They will have many troubles there, and they will not be free there. But I will rescue them, and they will come and live in this land."

10. A Baby at Last

Genesis 17 – 18; 21:1-7

Abram was nearly one hundred, and he and Sarai still had no children! But God reminded Abram that he had promised him a family. And he made a new promise:

"People from your family will be kings."

God gave them new names: Abraham, which means "father of many," and Sarah, which means "princess."

Then, one day, three men visited Abraham and Sarah. They were messengers from God — but Abraham and Sarah didn't know this.

One of the visitors made a promise:

"This time next year, Sarah will have a baby boy."

When she heard this, Sarah laughed because she did not believe him. "I am too old to have a baby!" she thought.

A few months later, Sarah became pregnant. A year later, she had a baby boy. She and Abraham were parents at last! Now Sarah laughed with happiness. God had kept his impossible promise! They called the baby Isaac, which means "he laughs."

Isaac grew up and married Rebekah. They had two sons: Esau and Jacob.

Abraham and Sarah's family was growing at last.

11. Jacob's Sneaky Trick

Genesis 25:27-34; 27:1-45

Esau and Jacob were Isaac and Rebekah's twin sons. Esau was born first and Jacob came second.

In those days, a father gave everything he had to his oldest son. So everyone expected that Esau would be given God's promises of a huge family, a land to live in, and God's blessing.

But before the twins were born, God told Rebekah that his promises would be given to Jacob, even though he was younger.

When they grew up, Esau was very hairy, and he loved hunting. Jacob was not so hairy, and he liked cooking.

One day, Esau came home from hunting very hungry and saw Jacob cooking a stew. "Give me some of that food," he demanded.

"I'll let you have my food if you let me have the promises from God," said Jacob. Esau agreed.

When Isaac got very old, his eyes stopped working. So Jacob used a trick to get the promises. Jacob dressed in his brother's clothes and put goatskin on his hands so that he seemed very hairy. When Isaac felt Jacob's hands and smelled the clothes, he thought Jacob was Esau. So he said to Jacob, "I am giving God's promises to you."

When Esau found out what Jacob had done, he was furious! Jacob had to run away from home. But he took God's promises with him — just as God had said would happen before he was born.

12. Jacob's Special Dream

Genesis 28:10-17; 32:28

As Jacob ran far, far away from his angry brother Esau, he stopped in a part of the land of Canaan to sleep.

God gave Jacob a special dream. He saw a stairway. The bottom was on the earth, and the top stretched up, up, up to heaven. Walking up and down the stairs were angels! And standing at the top was... God! And God said...

"I will give your family this land. It will be as hard to count all the people in your family as it is to count all the specks of dust in the world. I will use your family to bless people who live all over the earth — they will live under my rule and be happy in my world. I will look after you."

Jacob found it hard to remember God's promises and obey him. God gave him a nickname, "Israel," which means "wrestles with God." But God kept his promises. After many years, Jacob returned to live in the land where he had seen the stairway.

13. Joseph in Trouble

Genesis 37; 39; 50:20

Jacob had a big family. He had twelve sons. There was Reuben and Simeon and Levi. Then came Judah, Issachar and Zebulun, and Dan and Naphtali and Gad and Asher. Then came the sons he loved most: Joseph and Benjamin.

Because Jacob loved Joseph more than his brothers, he gave him a special coat. Joseph's brothers did not like this, and they started to not like Joseph.

Joseph had some dreams which showed that one day his brothers would bow down to him as their ruler. When he told his brothers about the dreams, they *really* did not like Joseph. So they made a plan.

Joseph's brothers sold him to some people who were on their way to the land of Egypt. They told Jacob that Joseph had been killed by a wild animal.

Joseph was made a slave. He had to work for someone else and was not free to make his own decisions. But he knew God was with him, and God helped him work hard.

Then it got worse. Joseph was put in prison. But even there, Joseph knew that God was looking after him. He knew that God had a plan.

14. Joseph and the King of Egypt

Genesis 40:1 – 41:43

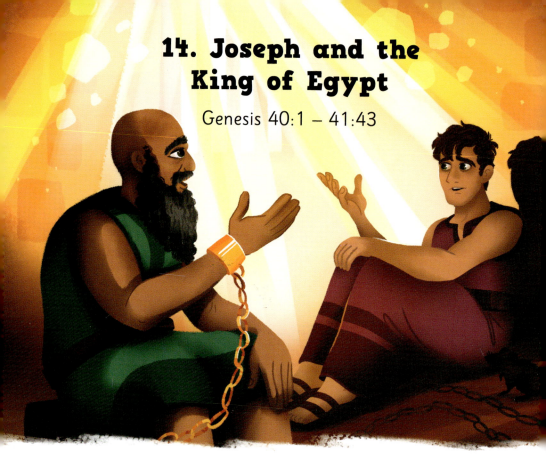

Joseph was in prison in Egypt. In the prison was a man whose job had been to choose the king's drinks for him. This man had a special dream. Joseph explained it to him: "You will be allowed out of prison and get your job back."

And that is exactly what happened.

Two years later, the king had some strange dreams — so the drink-chooser told him about Joseph.

The king fetched Joseph. "Can you tell me what my dreams mean?" he asked.

"God will give me the answer," Joseph replied.

"I dreamed about seven fat cows and seven skinny cows," the king said. "The skinny cows ate the fat ones!

"Next I dreamed about seven healthy and seven thin ears of grain. And the thin ears swallowed the healthy ears."

Joseph explained, "This is God's way of showing you the future. There will be seven years when lots of food grows – then seven years when no food grows at all.

"You will need to save lots of food for seven years," Joseph told the king, "so that people will have food to eat for the seven years after that."

The king was amazed. "God has shown all this to you," he said. "So I am putting you in charge of all of Egypt."

Joseph had started the day in prison. Now he was ruling a country!

15. Joseph Meets His Brothers
Genesis 42 – 46

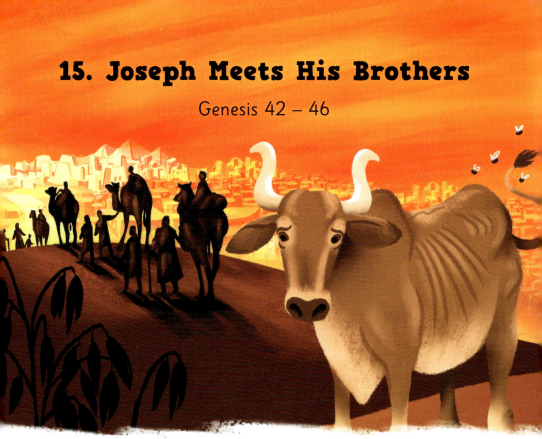

Joseph was in charge of Egypt. He saved up food for seven years so that when no food grew for seven years after that, people in Egypt still had enough to eat.

In Canaan lived Jacob and his sons. These were Joseph's brothers, who years and years before had sold him as a slave. No food grew in Canaan either, so there was nothing to eat. So Jacob's sons went to Egypt to ask for food.

In Egypt, the brothers met Joseph — but they did not know it was him! They bowed down and asked for food.

Joseph wanted to know if his brothers had changed since they had been so mean to him. So he hid his precious cup in his brother Benjamin's bag.

Then Joseph said, "Benjamin stole this cup! Now he will have to be my slave."

What would the brothers do?

One of them, Judah, stepped forward and said, "Please let Benjamin go free. I will be your slave instead of him."

Joseph knew now that his brothers had changed. "It's me!" he said. "I'm your brother Joseph!" And he explained that God had used everything that had happened to keep his promise to look after Jacob's family.

Jacob and his sons went to live in Egypt. Jacob's family grew and grew until it was very hard to count them all.

16. A Baby in the River

Exodus 1:1 – 2:10

A new king, or pharaoh, was in charge of Egypt. Jacob and Joseph had died, and this pharaoh did not like their family, who were called the Israelites.

So Pharaoh enslaved them. For their whole life, they had to work for him. There were no days off. They could not leave. They were not free.

And then, because Pharaoh *really* did not like the Israelites, he decided that every Israelite baby boy would be killed. God's people were in great danger.

One Israelite mother decided to hide her baby son. She put him in a basket and hid him in the reeds at the edge of the great River Nile.

Pharaoh's daughter went for a swim in the Nile and found... the baby boy! She decided to keep him and care for him. She called him Moses.

So Moses the Israelite was safe. He grew up as part of Pharaoh's family.

17. Moses and the Burning Bush

Exodus 2:11 – 3:17

Moses the Israelite grew up in Pharaoh's palace, but when he was older he chose the side of the Israelites, not the Egyptians. Pharaoh was so angry that Moses had to run away to live in a different country.

One day, Moses saw a bush that was on fire but was not burning up. He went closer to look – and a voice spoke!

"I am the God of your great-great-great-great-grandfathers Abraham, and Isaac, and Jacob," said the voice.

"I have seen that the Israelites are slaves in Egypt. I will rescue them.

I will show Pharaoh that I am much more powerful than him.

I will take them to the land that I promised Abraham, Isaac, and Jacob I would give their family.

And Moses, I will use you to do all of this."

Moses was not at all sure that this was possible. But God reminded Moses that he was the God who never changed, and that he could keep impossible promises.

Moses believed God's impossible promise and so he did as God said. He went back to Egypt to go and tell Pharaoh to let God's people go free.

18. Let My People Go!

Exodus 5:1-14; 7:14 – 10:29

Moses the Israelite went to see Pharaoh, just as God had told him to.

"God says, 'Let my people go!'"

And Pharaoh replied, "No!"

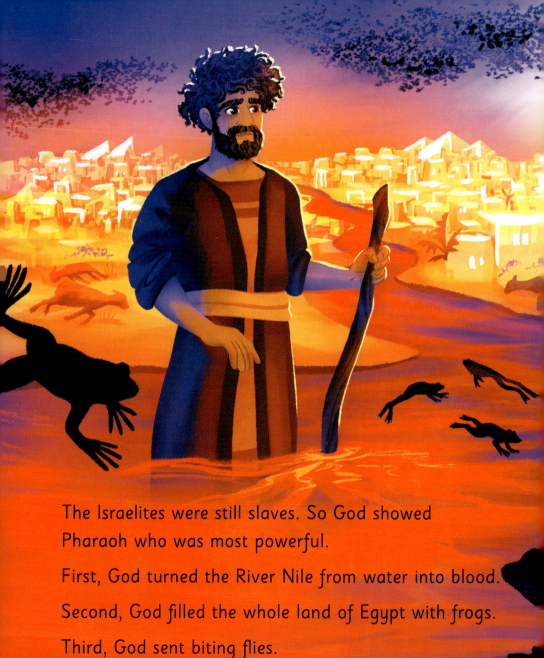

The Israelites were still slaves. So God showed Pharaoh who was most powerful.

First, God turned the River Nile from water into blood.

Second, God filled the whole land of Egypt with frogs.

Third, God sent biting flies.

Fourth, God sent swarms of flies that covered everything and everyone, apart from where the Israelites lived.

Fifth, God made all the animals that belonged to the Egyptians die.

Sixth, God made horrible, painful lumps grow on the Egyptians' skin.

Seventh, God sent a huge storm all over Egypt, apart from where the Israelites lived.

Eighth, God sent millions and millions of locusts, which ate every single plant.

Ninth, God made it go completely and utterly dark for three days, apart from where the Israelites lived.

Everything was ruined.

Moses went to see Pharaoh again.

"God says, 'Let my people go!'"

And Pharaoh replied, "No!"

The Israelites were still slaves. But God was not finished. He had one last way to show he was more powerful than Pharaoh.

19. The Rescue from Egypt

Exodus 12 – 13

It was time for God to rescue his people from being Pharaoh's slaves in Egypt.

He gave them these instructions: "Eat a lamb for dinner. Before you eat it, paint its blood around your front doors. Then be ready to leave Egypt straightaway.

"Tonight, the oldest son in each house in Egypt is going to die. But wherever I see blood around the front door, I will know a lamb has already died. I will pass over that house, and everyone in it will be safe."

The Israelites believed God's promise and so they did as God said.

That night, God did exactly what he'd promised. Every family with a lamb's blood painted around their front door was safe.

Moses went to see Pharaoh.

And Pharaoh said, "Go!"

So the Israelites left Egypt straightaway. There were so many of them that it was very hard to count them...

... and now they were all free.

20. A Path through the Sea

Exodus 14:5 – 15:21

After Pharaoh let Moses and the Israelites leave Egypt, he changed his mind. He wanted his slaves back! So he took his army to get them.

Pharaoh had hundreds and hundreds and hundreds of chariots. The Israelites had zero chariots.

Behind them, all the Israelites could see were Pharaoh's chariots. In front of them, all they could see was sea – and the Israelites had zero boats.

They were terrified.

God told Moses to hold out his staff. And God sent a super-strong wind that blew the sea into two water-walls with a dry path between them. The Israelites walked along the path to the other side of the sea.

The Egyptians chased them along the path. Then God told Moses to hold out his staff again, and this time the water-walls collapsed and the Egyptians were swept away.

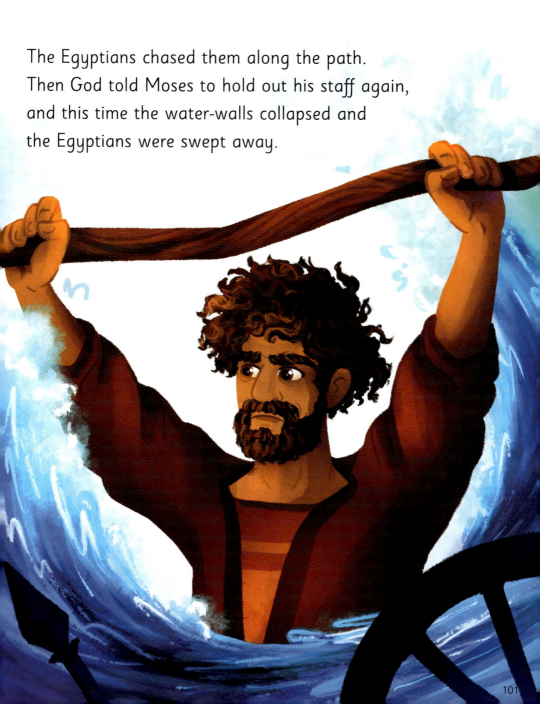

The Israelites stood on the shore and sang to God: "There is no one else like you. No one else can do what you do. You have rescued your people and you will bring us to our land. You are the greatest king."

21. God's Commands

Exodus 19:1 – 20:17; 24:3

After they left Egypt, the Israelites came to Mount Sinai.

Thunder rolled, lightning flashed, and a thick cloud covered the mountain. Then God appeared as a huge, blazing fire. This was his way of showing that he was making an unbreakable promise.

Moses went up Mount Sinai, and God gave him a message for all the Israelites:

"I have rescued you from Egypt. Now, obey me fully. And you will be my people – my special family."

To show the people how to obey him, God gave them Ten Commandments:

1. Don't worship any other God.
2. Don't treat something you have made as if it's God. It will always be a not-god.
3. Don't say God's name in a way that makes it seem he's not real or important.
4. Keep one day each week to rest and to spend time talking and listening to God.
5. Obey and love your parents.
6. Don't murder anyone.
7. Don't treat someone who is married to someone else as though they are married to you.
8. Don't take other people's things.
9. Don't say things that are not true.
10. Don't get annoyed that you don't have things that other people have.

God gave them lots of other ways to obey him too. And he promised to give them the land he had promised Abraham.

"We believe your promises and will do everything you've said," the Israelites replied.

22. God's Tent

Exodus 25 – 27; 40:34-38

While they were in the desert, the Israelites lived in tents. God wanted to live with them, so he told Moses how to build a special tent for him.

This tent would be in the middle of the camp, and in the middle of the tent would be the most special place in the world – the place where God lived among his people.

God told Moses to put a thick curtain in front of that most special place. It was like a big Keep Out sign. It showed the people that because they did not keep God's laws all the time, they did not deserve to be friends with God and live with him forever.

But then God said the people could burn a dead animal in front of his tent. God would see that an animal had died instead of the people, to take the punishment they deserved. Then they could be his friends and live with him forever.

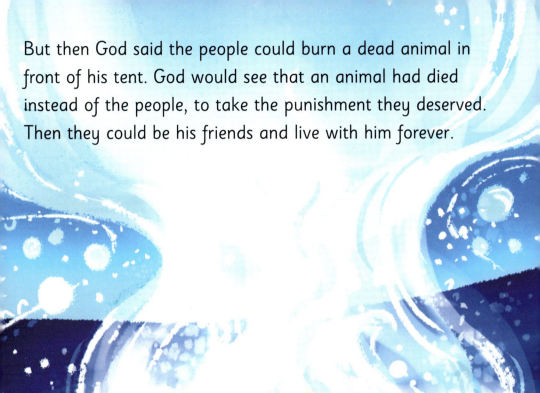

The Israelites built the tent exactly as God told them to. It was called the tabernacle. And God appeared as a cloud and came to live in it.

23. Making a Not-God

Exodus 32:1 – 33:17

While Moses was up on Mount Sinai talking with God, at the bottom of Mount Sinai the Israelites decided to make a new god – a not-god. So they made a calf out of gold and then had a big feast to celebrate their not-god.

When the real God saw what they were doing, he was angry. He told Moses...

"These people have not obeyed me. I will not be with them anymore. They cannot be my people or live in my land."

Moses pleaded with God: "These people are Abraham's family. Please choose to love them even though they have disobeyed you. Please let us be your people and live in your land. Please show everyone that you are the God who always keeps his promises, no matter what."

God was pleased with Moses. So he did not leave his people.

Moses went down the mountain and took the not-god apart. The Israelites who did not like him doing this died. God led the rest of them through the desert toward the land he had promised to Abraham.

24. Joshua, Caleb, and the Explorers

Numbers 13:1 – 14:35

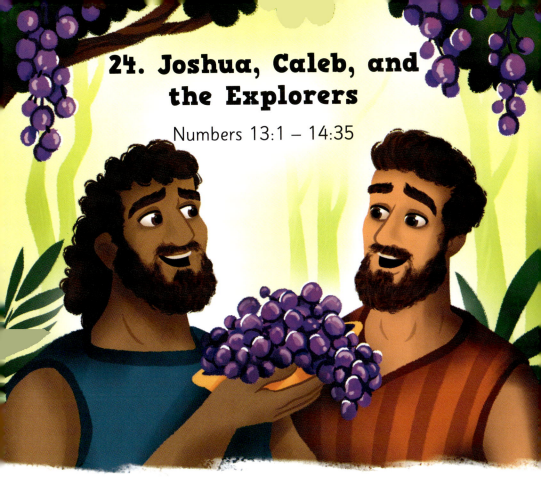

The Israelites had reached the edge of the land God had promised to give them. Moses sent twelve men to go and explore it.

When the explorers came back, they were carrying wonderful fruit. "It is an amazing place," they said.

"But..." ten of them added, "the people who live there are very big and very strong, and their cities are very big and very strong. We are too weak to take the land."

Two of the explorers disagreed.

"God is with us!" said Joshua and Caleb. "He will give us the land. We just need to believe in his promises. Let's go!"

But the people would not listen. They wailed, "Let's go back to Egypt" – even though they had been slaves there.

God was not pleased. He decided that the people who had not believed his promise would not be allowed into his land. Only their children, once they were grown up, would be able to go into the land.

"But I will let Joshua and Caleb enjoy living in my land," said God, "because they are the only ones who trust my promises and want to obey me."

25. Moses Sees the Land

Deuteronomy 18:17-20; 34

Moses had led the Israelites out of slavery in Egypt and had led them for forty years in the desert. Now he was about to die. He told the people that it was time for them to go into the land God had promised to give them.

He told them that after he had died, God wanted Joshua to be their leader. He reminded them to believe God's promises and always do as God said.

Before Moses died, he climbed up a massive mountain. He could see for miles and miles and miles, all the way to the sea. God said to him, "All the land you can see – all the way to the sea – is the land I will give the Israelites. I wanted you to see it before you die."

26. Rahab and the Explorers

Joshua 1 – 3

Joshua was the leader of the Israelites. God gave him a promise: "Lead the people into the land, and I will give you victory over everyone who lives there. Obey me and have courage, and I will be with you everywhere you go."

Joshua listened to God's promise and so he did as God said.

Joshua sent two men to explore the land. They went secretly to Jericho, a very big city with very, very big walls. But the king of Jericho found out they were there — and he sent soldiers to catch them.

Rahab lived in Jericho. She had heard how God had rescued the Israelites from Egypt, and she knew he was the real God. She decided to hide the explorers from the soldiers.

"When we take over Jericho, we will protect you and your family," the explorers promised her. Then they escaped back to Joshua. They were safe.

Joshua and all the Israelites crossed the River Jordan. God split the river into two water-walls and they walked across on a dry path. At long, long, long last, God's people were standing in the land that God had promised to give them.

27. The Walls of Jericho
Joshua 6

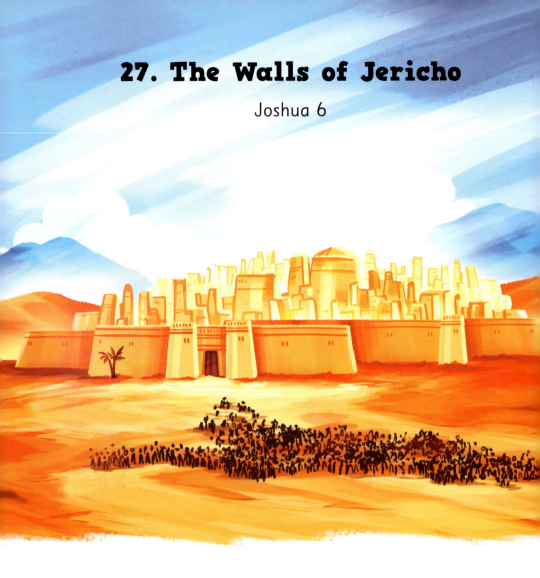

Joshua led the Israelites to Jericho, the very big city with the very, very big walls. The people who lived there locked their gates. There was no way to get in.

God told Joshua that all the soldiers should march around the city once every day for six days. Then, on day seven, they should march round seven times. The last time, they should blow their trumpets and shout.

God promised that when they did this, the very big walls would completely collapse.

Joshua did as God said. The Israelites marched around Jericho once. Twice. Three times. Four. Five. Six.

Then on day seven, seven times. Then they blew their trumpets and shouted.

At that moment the walls came crashing down.
God had given the Israelites the city!

The two explorers who Rahab had hidden went and found her and brought her and her family to live with the Israelites. She was safe.

28. Joshua Says Goodbye

Joshua 23:14 – 24:28

Joshua had led the Israelites in many battles and they had won many victories. Now the whole land belonged to them. They could live in houses and grow food and enjoy peace.

Joshua was old, so before he died he called the Israelites together to say goodbye.

"God has looked after us," Joshua reminded them. "God has made lots of promises to us – and he has kept every single one of them. Now you must obey God so that you can keep enjoying life in the land he has given us."

"Everyone has to choose whether to love and obey God or not," Joshua said. "I am choosing to love and obey God."

"We choose that too," said all the people.

So, for a while, all God's people lived happily, under his rule, in the land that he had given them.

29. Deborah, Barak, and the Big Battle

Judges 4 – 5

The Israelites were in big trouble.

After Joshua died, they kept forgetting about all that God had done for them. They kept failing to obey him and kept choosing to love not-gods.

So God kept letting their enemies defeat them.

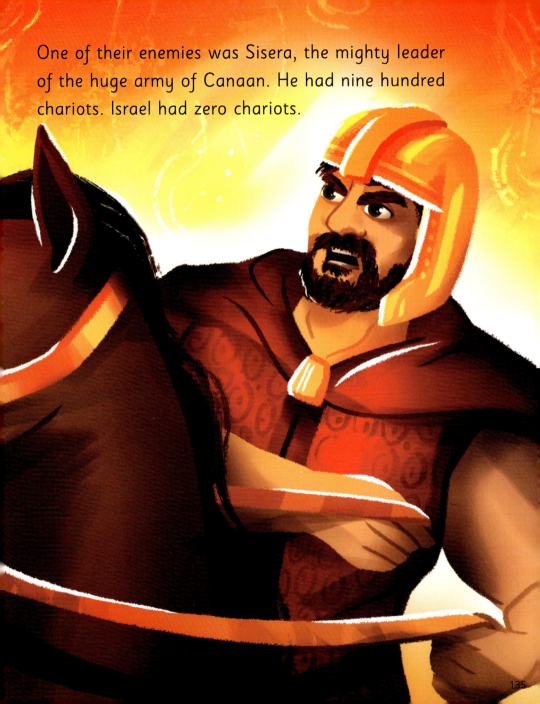
One of their enemies was Sisera, the mighty leader of the huge army of Canaan. He had nine hundred chariots. Israel had zero chariots.

The Israelites cried out to God to help them. So God gave them a leader called Deborah. She told them how to obey God.

Deborah told Barak, the not-so-mighty leader of the not-so-huge army of Israel, that it was time for battle.

"Go and fight!" Deborah told him. "God will give you victory over Sisera!"

So Barak fought. And God sent a storm to stop Sisera using his chariots so that the Israelite army could win the battle. God's people enjoyed freedom and peace again.

30. Samson Saves the Israelites

Judges 14 – 16

The Israelites were in big trouble (again). They had stopped obeying God (again). So God had let their enemies defeat them (again).

God gave his people a leader called Samson and gave him great strength to fight their enemies, the Philistines.

But Samson did not want to fight the Philistines. Instead, he fell in love with one of them. She was called Delilah.

The Philistine leaders promised Delilah, "Tell us the secret of Samson's great strength, and we will make you rich."

So Delilah asked Samson, "Why are you so strong?"

Samson would not tell. But Delilah asked again, and again, and again. At last Samson told her: "God made me strong, and I must show I am his servant by never cutting my hair. If my hair is cut off, I will lose my strength."

Delilah waited till Samson was asleep... and then cut his hair off. Philistine soldiers came to grab Samson, and now he was too weak to fight them.

Samson was thrown into prison. And his hair started to grow again.

One day, the Philistines were having a party. "Bring out Samson so we can laugh at him!" they shouted.

Out came Samson. He was standing next to the pillars that held the building's roof up. "God, make me strong one last time so that I can fight the Philistines," he prayed. He pushed the pillars as hard as he could...

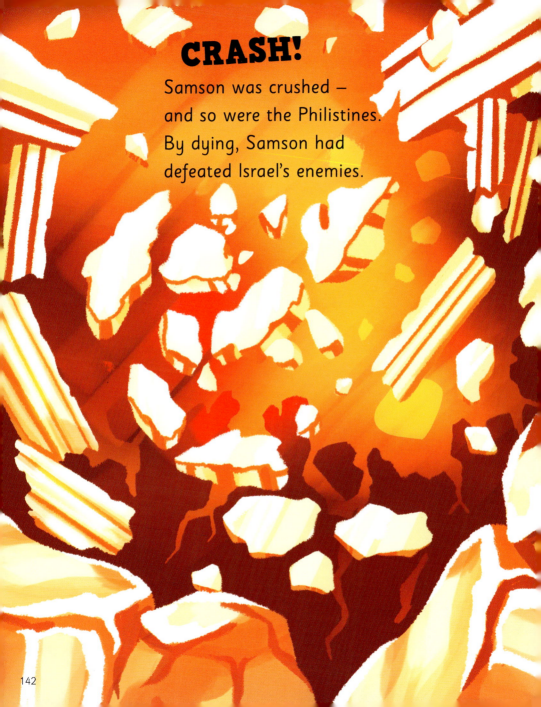

31. Ruth Finds a Family

Ruth

There was no food in Israel. Everyone was getting hungrier and hungrier. So a man called Elimelek decided to move to a country called Moab with his wife Naomi and their two sons. People in Moab did not love or obey God, and people from Israel and Moab did not like each other at all.

In Moab, Elimelek's sons married women called Orpah and Ruth. But Elimelek died. And then his sons died. Naomi, Orpah, and Ruth were all alone.

Naomi heard there was food again in Israel, so she decided to go back to Bethlehem, where she had lived.

"I will come with you," said Ruth. "From now on, I will love and obey the God who you love and obey."

When Naomi and Ruth arrived in Bethlehem, they had no money and no food. So Ruth went to a field to pick some leftover corn. The field belonged to Boaz, who was from the same family as Elimelek.

Boaz knew that Ruth and Naomi needed help, and he chose to take care of them. He made sure Ruth was safe and gave her lots of food.

Ruth and Boaz decided to get married. They had a baby boy called Obed. Naomi loved looking after him.

"Praise God!" said Naomi's friends. "He has given you a family again."

32. Hannah's Special Son

1 Samuel 1 – 2

Hannah was terribly sad. She wanted to be part of the way God kept his promises to fill the world with people and make Abraham's family huge. But she could not have any children.

One day, Hannah went to the tabernacle, the special tent where God lived among his people.

Hannah cried. And Hannah prayed: "Lord, I am so upset. Please give me a son, and then I will give him to you, to serve you for his whole life."

Eli worked in the tabernacle as the chief priest. He saw that something was wrong with Hannah. When she explained how sad she was, Eli said, "I hope God gives you what you have asked for."

Hannah felt much better when she had prayed.

God gave Hannah what she had asked – a son, called Samuel.

And Hannah gave God what she had promised. When Samuel was three years old, she took him to live with Eli and work with him in the tabernacle. When Samuel grew older, he became God's messenger to Israel.

Hannah prayed again:

"God, you have made my heart feel happy. There is no one else like you. You are kind to everyone who knows they need you."

33. We Want a King!

1 Samuel 8 – 13

Nahash was the fierce king of Ammon. The Israelites were scared of him and his army.

So they said to God's messenger Samuel, "We want a king to fight for us! We want a king like everyone else has!"

Samuel reminded the people that God was their king.

"If you choose a king like everyone else has, he will take your children to serve him, and he will take your land and animals to make himself rich," Samuel warned them. "You will soon be sad to have chosen a king who isn't God."

"No!" they insisted. "We want a king like everyone else!"

So God gave them what they had chosen. He gave them a king called Saul.

Saul was very tall — and the people were pleased about that. Saul defeated Nahash — and the people were pleased about that too.

But Saul did not obey God – and God was not pleased about that.

God decided that Saul would not be king much longer. Instead, he would give Israel the king they needed, instead of the king they wanted. Who would he choose?

34. God Chooses a King
1 Samuel 16

One day God sent his messenger Samuel to visit Jesse, a man who lived in Bethlehem. Jesse's grandparents were Ruth and Boaz. "I have chosen one of Jesse's sons to be the next king of Israel," God told Samuel.

When Samuel arrived, he saw Jesse's son Eliab. Samuel thought Eliab looked like a king.

But God said to Samuel, "You care about what people look like, but I care about what someone is really like, on the inside. I have not chosen Eliab to be king."

Next came Jesse's son Abinadab. God did not choose him. Then came Shammah. God did not choose him. Then came four more sons. God did not choose any of them.

"Do you have any more sons?" Samuel asked Jesse.

"I have one more, the youngest," answered Jesse. "He is out looking after the sheep." Jesse sent someone to fetch him.

His name was David. When David came in, God told Samuel, "This is the one I have chosen."

So Samuel poured oil over David's head to show that he would be the next king.

And God poured his Spirit into David to make him ready to be the next king.

35. David and Goliath
1 Samuel 17

The Israelites were in big trouble. The Philistines had attacked, and the Philistines had a hero — a huge, huge, huge soldier called Goliath. He was nearly as tall as one normal man standing on another normal man's shoulders.

"I will fight any of you," Goliath shouted at the Israelite army. "If I lose, we will be your slaves. But if I win, you will be our slaves."

The Israelites were too scared to fight Goliath. Even King Saul was too scared.

David's big brothers were Israelite soldiers. One day he visited them and heard Goliath shouting.

"I will go and fight him," said David.

Goliath's clothes were made of metal and weighed the same as seventeen bricks.

David just wore a cloak.

Goliath had a massive sword and a monstrous spear and a mighty shield.

David had a small sling and five stones.

When Goliath saw David, he laughed.

David answered, "You have weapons, but I have God. God will give me victory over you."

David hurled a stone from his sling...

It hit Goliath.

And down he fell.

Dead.

The Israelites chased the Philistines as they ran away. God's people were not scared anymore – Goliath was dead, David had won, and now they were free!

36. A King Forever

2 Samuel 5 – 7; Psalm 51

David became king of Israel. God gave David victory over all the enemies of God's people... a new city to live in, called Jerusalem... and the ability to write lots of songs about God and his people, called psalms.

The people lived under God's rule and were happy in the land he had given them.

One day, God gave King David a promise: "One of your children will become king after you. And someone from your family will become a king forever. He will be like a son to me, and I will always love him."

David answered with a big thank-you prayer: "God, you are great. There is no one else like you. You have made Israel your special people, and you have been super, super kind to me. Thank you for your promises."

David was a great king, though sometimes he made big mistakes. But when he did, he said to God...

"I know that I have not obeyed you. I don't deserve to be your friend. I am sorry. Please forgive me so that I can still enjoy being your friend, and please change me so I can obey you as I should."

37. King Solomon

1 Kings 3:1 – 11:13

Solomon became king of Israel when his father David died.

"I want to rule your people well, God," Solomon prayed. "Please make me wise."

"I will make you the wisest person in the world," answered God.

Solomon built a temple in Jerusalem. He used stone and wood and gleaming gold and dazzling jewels. In the middle of the temple was the most special place in the world — the place where God lived among his people.

Because Solomon was so wise and so rich, the queen of Sheba went on a long journey to visit him. "This land is amazing!" she said. "Everyone must be very happy to have such a good king. God must love his people very much."

But then Solomon stopped being wise, and decided to worship not-gods instead of the real God. God was not pleased. "Because you have stopped loving me, your son will not rule over Israel," he said. "But I promised your father David that his family would rule my people. So I will let your son be king of a small part of this land."

38. Things Go Very Wrong

1 Kings 12:1-33; 15:9-24

After Solomon died, God's people needed a new king. Rehoboam was Solomon's son, and he wanted to be ruler. He decided that being mean to God's people was the way to show his power.

Lots of people did not want a mean king, so they chose a different king called Jeroboam. He ruled over most of Israel, and Rehoboam ruled only a small part, called Judah. God's land was split into two parts.

The temple where God lived among his people was in Judah, and King Jeroboam did not want people to visit it. So he made up two not-gods and told the people he ruled to worship them instead of God. And they did. Soon, the people in Judah chose to love not-gods too.

Israel and Judah had king after king after king. Some were good, and told the people to love and obey God. Most were bad, and told the people to worship not-gods.

God sent lots of messengers to remind the kings and the people to believe his promises and obey his commands. But they chose not to listen. Things had gone very wrong.

39. Elijah and the Fire

1 Kings 16:29 – 17:1;
18:16-45

When Ahab and Jezebel were king and queen, they told everyone to worship the not-god Baal. They said Baal was super powerful. They said Baal made food grow.

God's messenger was called Elijah. "God will stop it raining," he warned King Ahab. "No food will grow."

And for years, no rain came and no food grew.

"You should worship and love God," Elijah told the people. But they were not sure whether to listen to him or Ahab.

So Elijah set a challenge. He put a dead bull on top of some wood and stones, and some men who worshipped Baal did the same. "Whichever God can set a bull on fire is the God you should love and obey," Elijah said to the people.

The men who worshipped Baal shouted and danced. They asked Baal to send fire. They *begged* Baal to send fire.

Nothing happened.

Elijah prayed to God: "Please show everyone that you are the real God, so that they will love and obey you again."

And...

FIRE! The bull was burned up, the wood was burned up — even the stones were burned up!

"This is the real God!" the people said.

And God sent rain so that food would grow again.

40. A King Is Coming

Isaiah

God's people in both Israel and Judah were in big trouble. Their enemies kept defeating them.

One of God's messengers was Isaiah. Isaiah brought a warning for the kings and the people:

"You have stopped believing God's promises. You have stopped loving and obeying God, and stopped loving each other. You have worshipped made-up not-gods.

"Soon God will not let you live in his land. You will be made to go somewhere else and be ruled by other people.

"All God's promises will be undone."

But Isaiah also brought a promise for the kings and the people:

"One day the king you need will come to rescue you.

He will be God himself, living with you.

He will be from David's family, and he will rule you perfectly.

He will take the punishment you deserve for not loving and obeying God.

And then he will rule as king forever.

"When this king comes…

    Wolves will be friends with sheep.

    Blind people will be able to see.

    People who can't walk will skip and jump.

    Dead people will come back to life.

    There will be nothing that's bad, so no one will ever feel sad.

"When this king comes, all God's promises will come true. Life will be better than ever before."

41. Jonah and the Big Fish

Jonah

One day God told Jonah to go to the powerful city of Nineveh with a message: "God is going to punish you for not loving him and not loving other people."

Jonah did not like the people of Nineveh. So he did not like the idea that they might listen to him and be sorry, and that God would forgive them and not punish them.

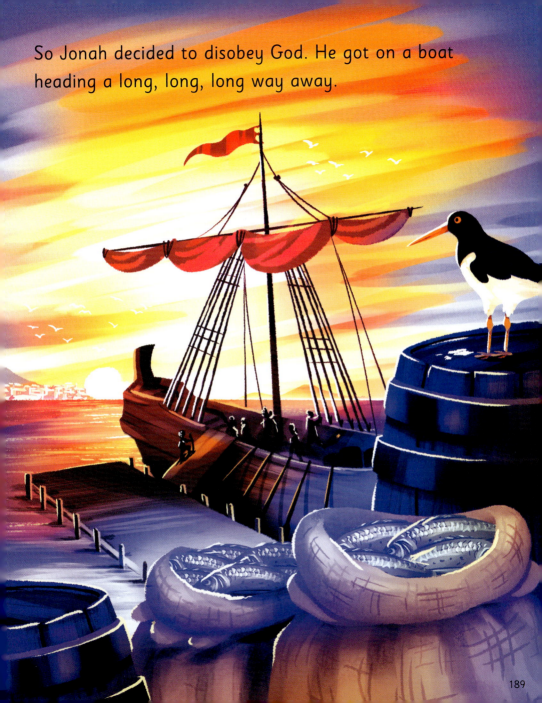

So Jonah decided to disobey God. He got on a boat heading a long, long, long way away.

But God sent a storm to stop Jonah. When the sailors on the boat found out what Jonah had done, they threw him into the sea.

Down,

down,

down

Jonah went...

... but God sent a big fish to swallow him.

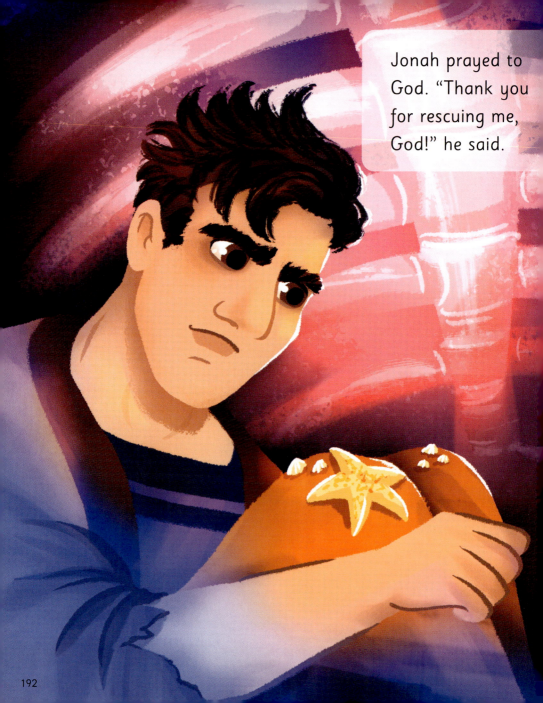

Jonah was inside the fish for three days and nights, and then God made it spit him out onto dry land.

Again, God told Jonah to go to Nineveh. This time Jonah obeyed. When they heard God's message, the king of Nineveh and all the people were very sorry. They changed how they lived. They hoped God would forgive them.

And God did.

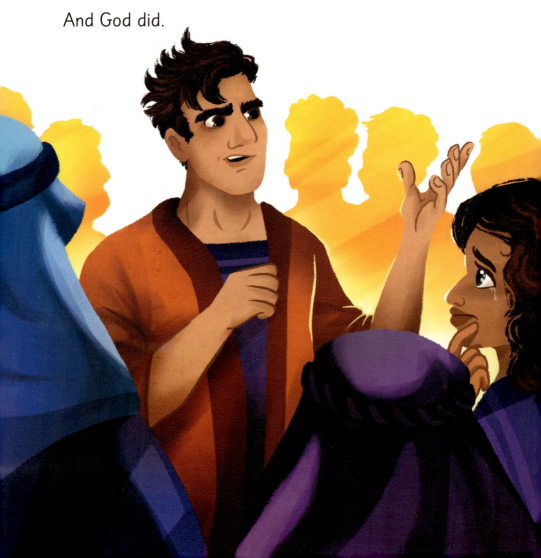

Jonah was very annoyed. But God was very pleased. "You care most about things that keep you comfortable," God told Jonah. "But I care most about people."

42. Out of the Land

2 Kings 17; 24:8-16; Ezekiel

Hoshea was king of Israel. He did not love or obey God. The people were the same.

God sent lots of messengers to warn them that if they chose to disobey him, he would choose to make them leave the land. But no one would listen.

So God let the mighty king of Assyria defeat the king of Israel. The people had to leave the land and go and live as strangers in Assyria.

Jehoiachin was king of Judah. He did not love or obey God. The people were the same.

So God let the mighty king of Babylon defeat the king of Judah. The temple in Jerusalem where God had lived among his people was destroyed, and the people had to leave the land and go and live as strangers in Babylon.

There, the people were sadder than they had ever been.

Ezekiel was one of God's messengers. "God says, 'I kept my promise that you would have to leave my land,'" he told the people. "'But now I promise to rescue you and bring you back to the land. I will keep that promise too.

"'I will give you the king you need. And I will send my Spirit to live in you. He will help you to obey me.'"

43. Daniel in the Lions' Den

Daniel 6

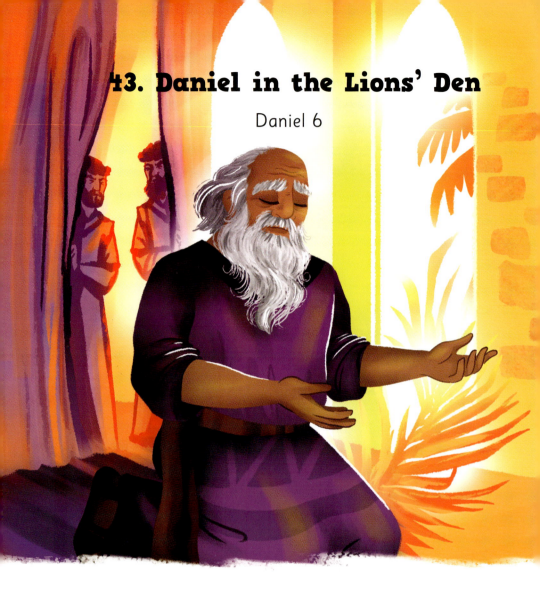

Daniel lived in Babylon. He worked for the king, and he loved God. He prayed to God every day.

Some other men who worked for the king wanted to get Daniel into trouble. So they said to the king...

"We think you should say that everyone must pray to you, and not to God. Anyone who does not obey you should be thrown into a den full of hungry lions."

So that is what the king commanded.

The men peeked into Daniel's house... and there he was, praying to God. They told the king. The king liked Daniel, but he couldn't change what he had said.

Daniel was thrown into the den of hungry lions.

That night, the king couldn't sleep. But that night, the lions didn't eat.

So when the king went to the den in the morning, there was Daniel – still alive!

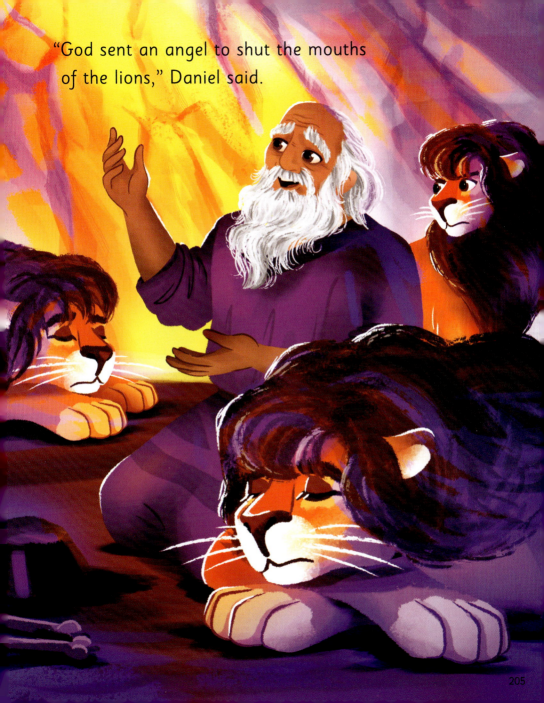

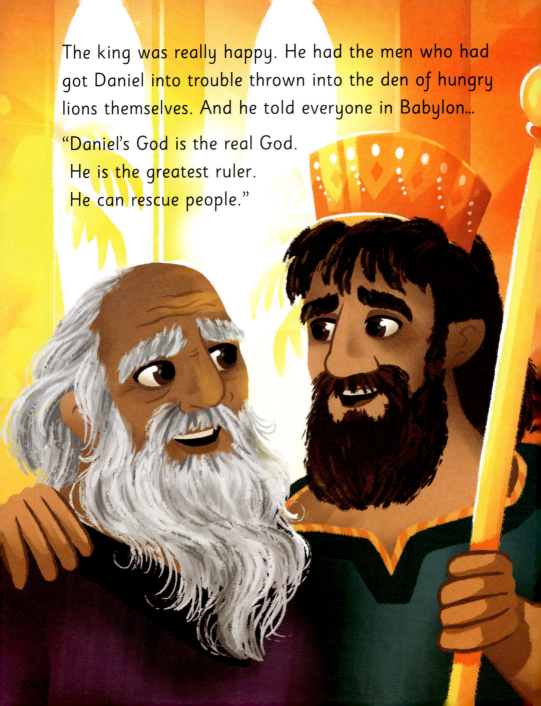

The king was really happy. He had the men who had got Daniel into trouble thrown into the den of hungry lions themselves. And he told everyone in Babylon...

"Daniel's God is the real God.
He is the greatest ruler.
He can rescue people."

44. The Brave Queen

Esther

When a man called Xerxes was the king of Persia and Babylon, he wanted a new queen. He told all the most beautiful women in his kingdom to come to his palace.

Esther was one of God's people, and she was very beautiful. When Xerxes saw her, he liked her the most. So Esther became his queen.

The king's chief servant was called Haman. He hated God's people. He came up with a nasty, crafty plan to get rid of them all. God's people were in big, big trouble.

Esther's Uncle Mordecai found out about Haman's plan. He asked Esther to go and speak to the king about it. This was very dangerous because the queen was not allowed to go and speak to the king unless he invited her to.

"But you have the chance to rescue God's people," Mordecai told Esther. "You might have become queen for this exact reason."

Esther was brave. She went to see the king... and he was pleased to see her. Esther told the king about Haman's nasty, crafty plan.

The king was angry with Haman. He got rid of Haman and gave his job to Mordecai. All God's people celebrated. Because Queen Esther was brave, they were safe!

45. Back in the Land Again

Ezra; Nehemiah; Malachi 3:1

Cyrus was king of Persia and Babylon. He was the most powerful ruler in the world. Cyrus decided to let God's people go home to the land God had given them. He told them that they could rebuild the temple in Jerusalem.

Zerubbabel was from the family of the kings of Judah. He went back with lots of the people. They rebuilt the temple.

Over many years, more and more of the people came back. Ezra made sure the people knew God's unbreakable promises and how to obey him. Nehemiah helped the people build a wall around the city to keep the people safe.

But the people were sad that not all of God's promises had come true. And they were not very good at obeying God. So God sent more messengers. One of them was Malachi.

"God says, 'I am coming,'" Malachi told them. "God says, 'I will send one last messenger, and then the one who will keep all my unbreakable promises will arrive.'"

So the people had to wait... and wait... and wait...

46. An Angel Visits Mary

Luke 1:26-38

Hundreds of years had passed since God had spoken to his people. Then, one day, he sent an angel to a little town called Nazareth and to a young woman called Mary. The angel was named Gabriel, and he had a message.

Mary had never seen an angel before. She was scared.

"Don't be afraid, Mary," said Gabriel. "God has chosen you for a very special job. You are going to have a baby boy called Jesus. He will be God's Son, he will be the king of God's people, and he will rule forever."

Mary asked the angel how she could have a baby whose father was God. It was impossible.

"God's Holy Spirit will make this happen," Gabriel answered. "God always keeps his promises."

"I am God's servant," replied Mary. "I am ready for all this to happen."

47. The Angel Speaks to Joseph

Matthew 1:18-25

Mary was planning to marry Joseph. Joseph was from the family that the great King David had been part of, hundreds and hundreds of years before.

When Joseph found out that Mary was having a baby and that he was not the baby's father, he felt very sad. He decided that he didn't want to marry Mary anymore.

So God sent an angel into one of Joseph's dreams.

"Joseph, you should still marry Mary," said the angel. "God's Holy Spirit has put this baby boy inside her. Call him Jesus, because he will rescue his people."

The angel said this because the name "Jesus" means "God rescues." Hundreds of years before, God's messenger Isaiah had said that all this would happen. God was coming to live with his people – as a person.

Joseph believed God's angel and so he obeyed what the angel had said. Joseph and Mary got married.

48. Mary's Thank-You Song

Luke 1:39-55

Mary went to see one of her relatives, called Elizabeth. Elizabeth had never been able to have children, and she was very old — but now she was pregnant! God had given a son to her and her husband Zechariah.

When Elizabeth saw Mary, Elizabeth's baby jumped inside her. It was her baby's way of showing that he knew that Mary's baby was very special.

"God has been very kind to you, Mary," said Elizabeth. "God is going to keep all his promises to you!"

Mary sang a thank-you song about God:

"God is amazing!
I'm so happy, because God is my rescuer and he cares for me.
I'm not special or strong, but I'm part of God's story.
God is good to everyone who knows that he is God.
God is kind to everyone who knows that they need him.
God is keeping all the promises that he has made."

49. Jesus Is Born

Luke 2:1-18

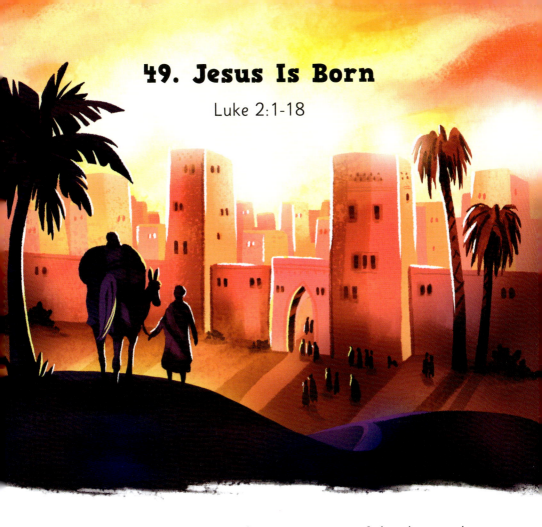

The Roman emperor was the most powerful ruler in the world. He wanted to count all the people he ruled over, so he ordered everyone to go to the town that their family was from. Even though Mary was about to have her baby, she and Joseph had to travel to Bethlehem.

In Bethlehem, Mary's baby was born. She named him Jesus. Because there was nowhere else for him to sleep, Mary wrapped Jesus in cloths and put him in a manger, where animal food was kept.

In some fields nearby, some shepherds were looking after their sheep. It was a dark night... and then suddenly everything was bright light... and an angel was there!

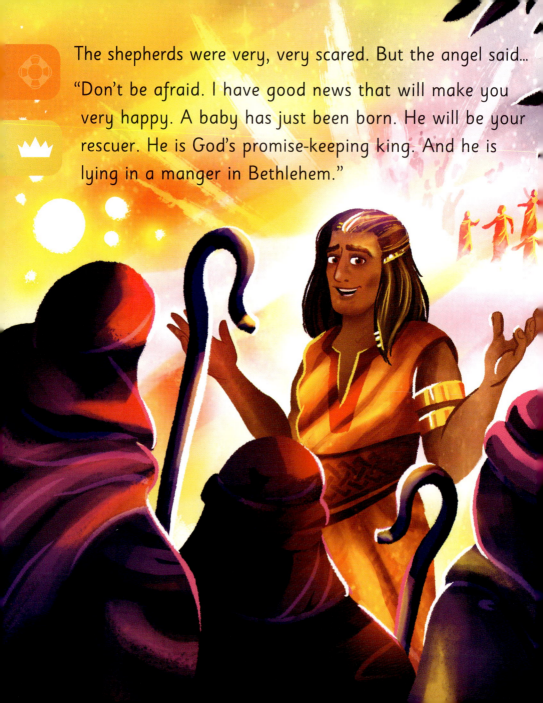

The shepherds were very, very scared. But the angel said...

"Don't be afraid. I have good news that will make you very happy. A baby has just been born. He will be your rescuer. He is God's promise-keeping king. And he is lying in a manger in Bethlehem."

Suddenly there were lots and LOTS of angels, singing songs about God.

"God is being praised by everyone in heaven, because he's bringing peace to his people on earth!" they sang.

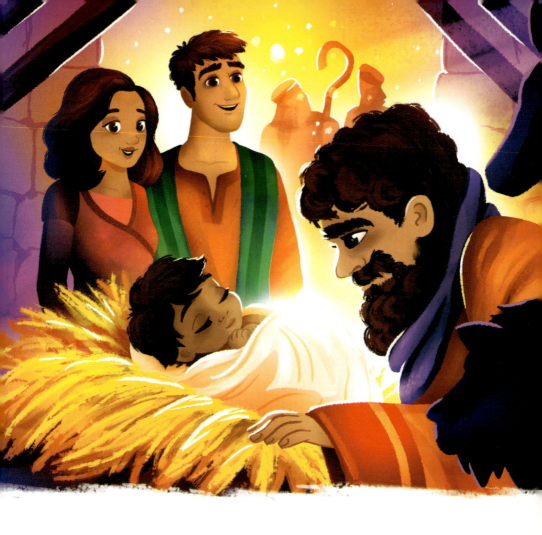

When the angels went back to heaven, the shepherds hurried to Bethlehem. They found the baby Jesus in a manger, just as the angel had said. Then they went and told everyone they could find about this promised, special baby.

50. Simeon and Anna Meet Jesus

Luke 2:22-39

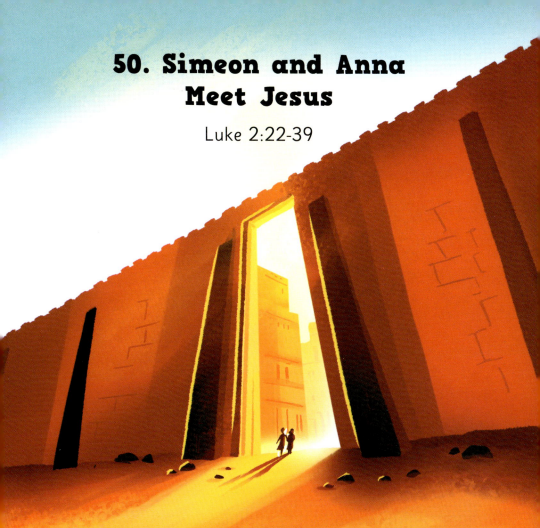

Joseph and Mary took baby Jesus to the temple in Jerusalem to say thank you to God for him. In Jerusalem lived an old, old man called Simeon. God's Holy Spirit had shown Simeon that he would see God's promise-keeping king before he died.

That day, God's Spirit sent Simeon to the temple. When he saw Jesus, Simeon took him in his arms and said...

"All-powerful God, you have kept your promise. I am looking at the way you will rescue your people. I am looking at the way you will bring joy to people who live all over the world."

As Simeon spoke, an old, old woman called Anna heard him. She was a messenger of God. She thanked God for Jesus, and she talked all about him to everyone who was looking forward to seeing God keep his promises.

51. Wise Men Arrive

Matthew 2:1-11

One day, some wise men who lived a long, long way from Bethlehem saw a new star in the sky. They knew that it meant God's promise-keeping king had been born.

The most important city in the land that God had given his people was Jerusalem — so the wise men headed there to find the baby king. But he wasn't there.

The king in Jerusalem was Herod, and he was not a child. Herod found some people who knew about God's promises and asked: "Where will God's promise-keeping king be born?"

"God said this king would be born in Bethlehem," they answered. So Herod told the wise men to look there. "As soon as you find him, let me know where he is," he ordered.

The wise men set off for Bethlehem. They saw the star again, which guided them to the place where Jesus was. They bowed down to Jesus and gave him presents: gold, frankincense, and myrrh.

52. Jesus Escapes
Matthew 2:12-23

The wise men were very happy to have found the king in Bethlehem. But God gave them a dream that warned them not to let King Herod know where Jesus was. So they went home without seeing Herod again.

After the wise men had left, God sent an angel into one of Joseph's dreams. "Herod does not want to let Jesus stay alive," the angel said. "Get up and take Jesus to Egypt."

Joseph believed the angel and so he obeyed what he said. He, Mary, and Jesus left Bethlehem as fast as they could, in the middle of the night, and went to live in Egypt.

When Herod found out that the wise men had gone home without telling him where Jesus was, he was very angry. But he was too late. Jesus was safe.

Jesus lived in Egypt with Joseph and Mary until Herod died and it was safe to come home. Then they went back to Nazareth, and Jesus grew older, and bigger, and smarter.

53. The Baptism of Jesus

Matthew 3:1-17

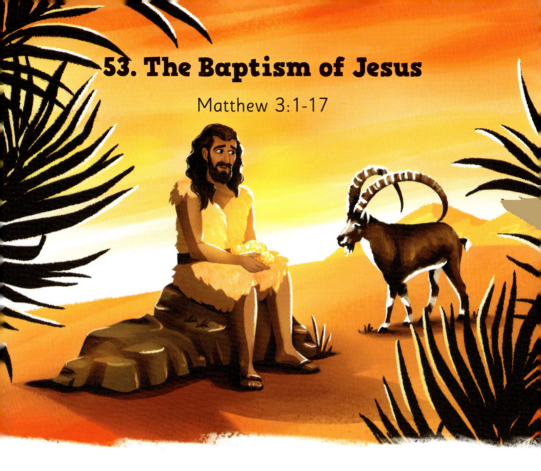

John the Baptist was Elizabeth's son and Jesus' relative. He had been given a very special job by God: to be the messenger who got people ready for God himself to arrive.

When John grew up, he lived in the desert. He ate locusts and honey, and he wore clothes made from camel's hair.

Lots of people came to listen to John. "You should be sorry that you have not loved and obeyed God," he told them. "Start living with God as your king again." If anyone was sorry, John washed them with water to show that they were making a new start – a clean start. This was called baptism.

"Someone greater than me is coming," John said. "I pour this water over you. He will pour God's Spirit into you."

One day, Jesus came to the river where John was baptizing people. "This is the person I have been telling you about!" John announced.

Jesus asked John to baptize him. When Jesus was in the water, God's Spirit came to him, looking like a dove. Then a voice spoke from heaven: "This is my Son," said God. "I love him, and I am very pleased with him."

54. Jesus in the Desert

Matthew 4:1-10

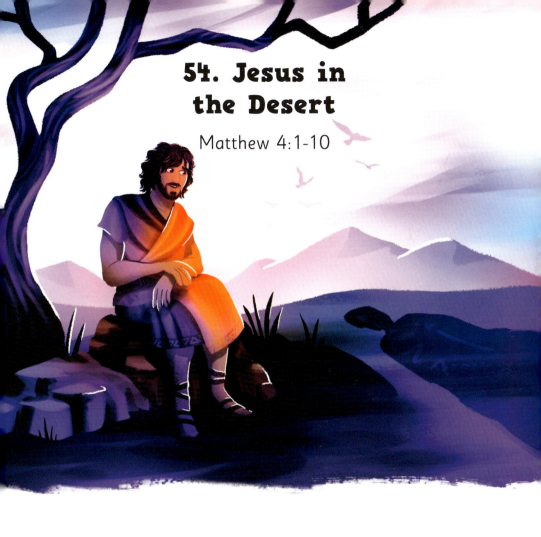

Jesus was in the desert on his own. The devil came to talk to him. The devil did not like God, he did not want to live under God's rule, and he had a bad plan. His plan was to get Jesus to choose not to obey God.

Jesus had been in the desert for forty days, so he was very hungry.

"If you really are God's Son, why don't you turn these stones into bread to eat?" said the devil.

"No," replied Jesus. "My Father would not want me to do that."

"If you really are God's Son, you could jump off a tall building, and God will tell his angels to catch you," said the devil. "Then everyone will know how great you are."

"No," replied Jesus. "God's word says that we should love God, not test God."

"I would like to give you everything in this world," said the devil. "Look at all the kingdoms and all the money and all the things. You can have it all... if you worship me."

"No," replied Jesus. "God's word says we should worship God and no one else."

The devil's plan had not worked. Jesus had obeyed his Father perfectly.

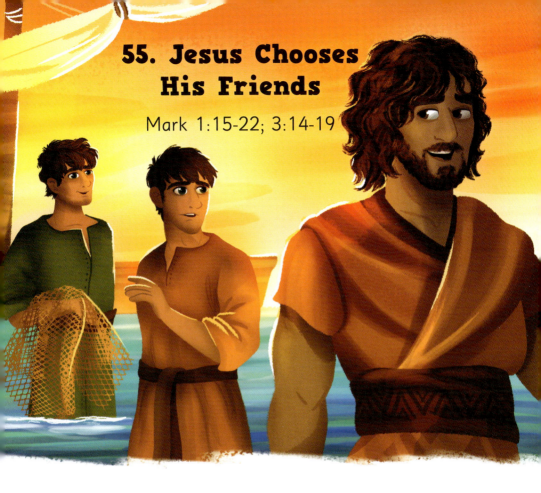

55. Jesus Chooses His Friends

Mark 1:15-22; 3:14-19

Jesus was walking by the sea when he saw two brothers going fishing. They were called Simon and Andrew.

"Come and follow me," said Jesus. "Instead of finding fish to be eaten by people, I will teach you to find people to be friends with me."

Simon and Andrew left their fishing nets straight away and followed Jesus. Then Jesus told two more fishermen, James and John, to follow him too – and they did.

Soon Jesus had picked twelve special friends to follow him and learn from him and tell people about him. As well as the four fishermen, Jesus chose Philip, Bartholomew, Matthew, Thomas, another James, Thaddeus, Simon the fighter, and Judas.
They were called Jesus' disciples. Jesus gave Simon the fisherman a new name: Peter.

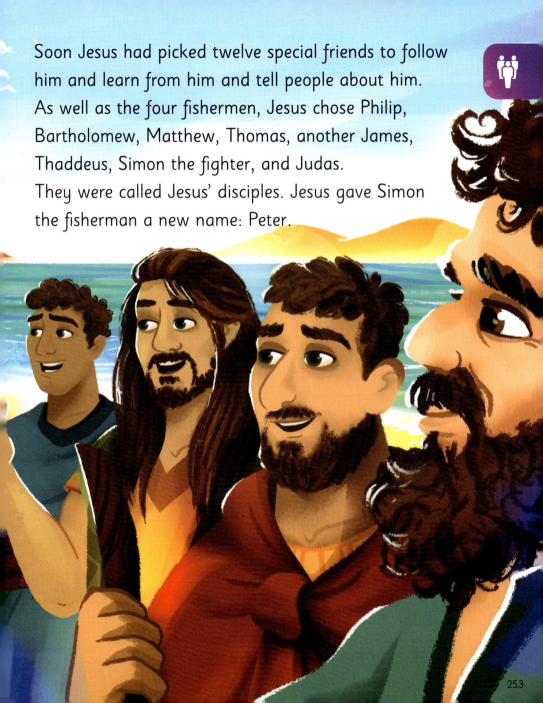

Jesus started telling people his message: "This is a special time," he said. "Because I have arrived, people can be part of God's kingdom. You need to love and obey me as your king and believe that I make all God's promises come true."

56. Get Up!
Luke 5:17-26

Jesus was teaching in a house. Because everyone wanted to listen to him, the house was stuffed full of people.

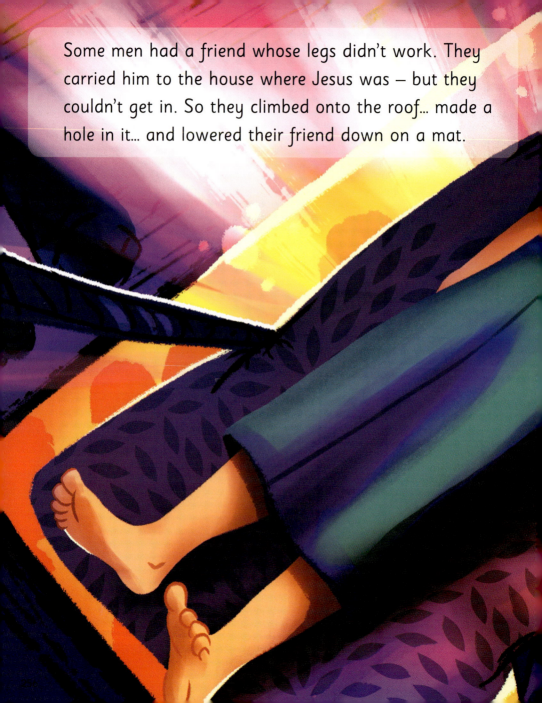

Some men had a friend whose legs didn't work. They carried him to the house where Jesus was — but they couldn't get in. So they climbed onto the roof... made a hole in it... and lowered their friend down on a mat.

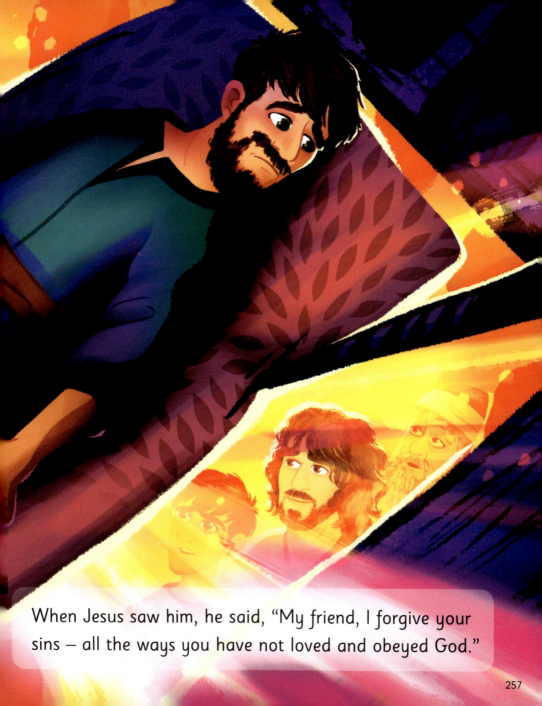

When Jesus saw him, he said, "My friend, I forgive your sins – all the ways you have not loved and obeyed God."

Some religious teachers who were there were annoyed. "Only God can forgive sins against him," they grumbled. "It is impossible for Jesus to do it. Does he think he is God?"

Jesus said, "Which is easier: to forgive this man's sins or to fix his legs? I will show you that I have power to forgive sins by doing something else that you think is impossible."

He told the man, "Get up!"

And he did!

The man thanked God – and so did everyone else, saying, "We have seen something amazing!"

57. A Dead Man Lives

Luke 7:11-16

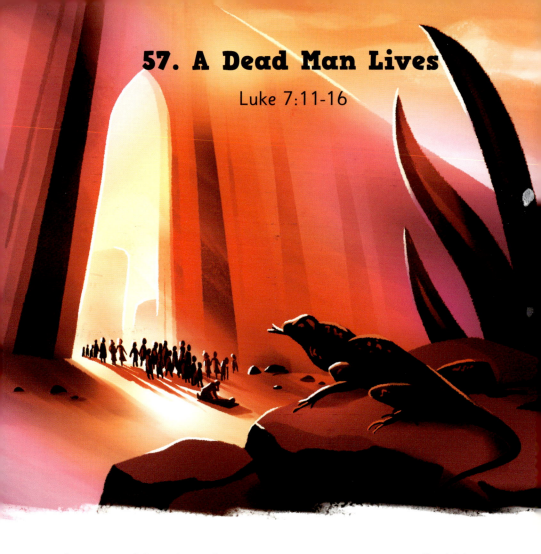

Jesus and his disciples were visiting a town called Nain. They saw a woman who was crying because her son had died and she was going to bury him. Lots of people were with her, and some of them were carrying her son's body.

When Jesus saw this woman, he felt so sad deep down inside that his tummy hurt.

"Don't cry," he told her. He touched her son's body. "Young man, I tell you to get up!" Jesus said.

And he did!

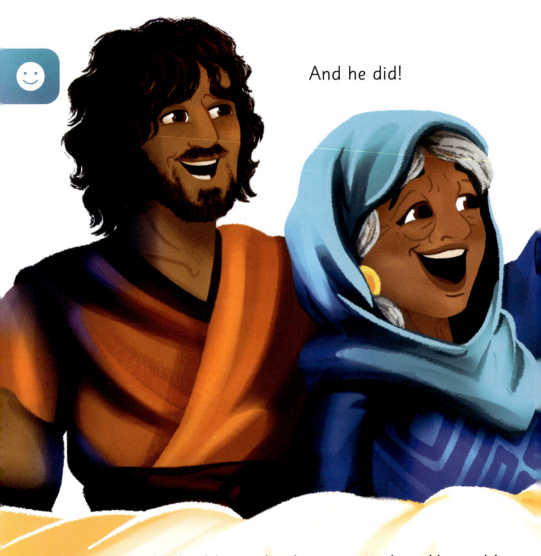

The man who had been dead was now alive. He could talk. He could walk. Everyone was amazed. "Jesus is a great messenger from God," they said. "Jesus is God's way of coming to help his people."

58. John the Baptist's Question
Luke 3:19-20; 7:18-28

King Herod's son was now the ruler. His name was Herod too. This Herod did not like what John the Baptist was teaching – so he put him in prison.

While he was in prison, John heard about the things Jesus was doing and saying. He wondered, "Is Jesus God's promise-keeping king? Or should we wait for someone else?" So he sent some of his friends to ask Jesus.

Jesus reminded John's friends of what God's messenger Isaiah had said hundreds of years before, about what God's promise-keeping king would do when he arrived.

"I have made blind people see," Jesus said. "I have fixed the legs of people who can't walk. I have brought dead people back to life. I have told people the good news that God has come to rescue them."

Then Jesus told the crowd of people with him: "John is doing something great, because he is a great messenger from God. But if you live with me as king, you are part of something even greater than that."

59. Jesus and the Storm

Mark 4:35-41

Jesus and his friends were crossing a huge lake on a boat. Jesus was very tired, so he put his head on a cushion and fell asleep.

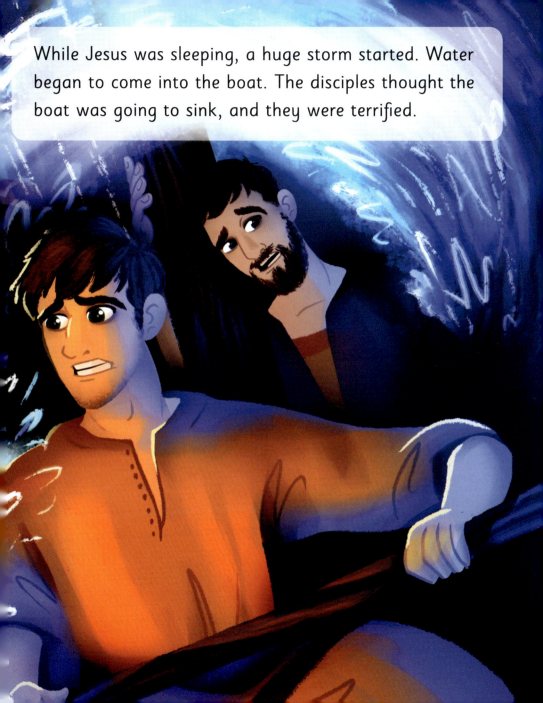

While Jesus was sleeping, a huge storm started. Water began to come into the boat. The disciples thought the boat was going to sink, and they were terrified.

And they were! The storm stopped completely.

Jesus said to his disciples, "You did not need to be scared. You need to believe in me."

His friends were amazed. "Even the wind and the waves obey Jesus," they told each other. "So who is he? He must be..."

60. Come Out of Him!
Mark 5:1-20

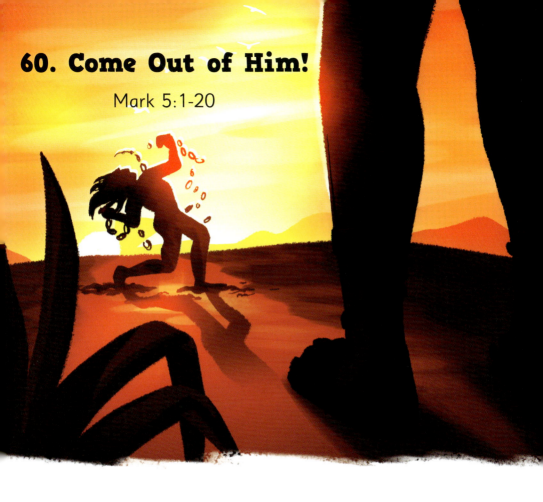

Jesus and his friends landed their boat on a beach. There they met a man who was in big trouble. Some evil spirits had made his life very miserable. He felt mixed up inside. He was nasty to anyone who tried to help, he tore his clothes, and he had to live far away from other people.

When this man saw Jesus, he shouted, "What are you going to do, Jesus, Son of the mighty God? Don't hurt me!"

Jesus didn't want to hurt him – he wanted to help him. He said to the evil spirits, "Come out of him!"

He sent the evil spirits into some pigs on a nearby hill. The pigs rushed down the slope into the lake.

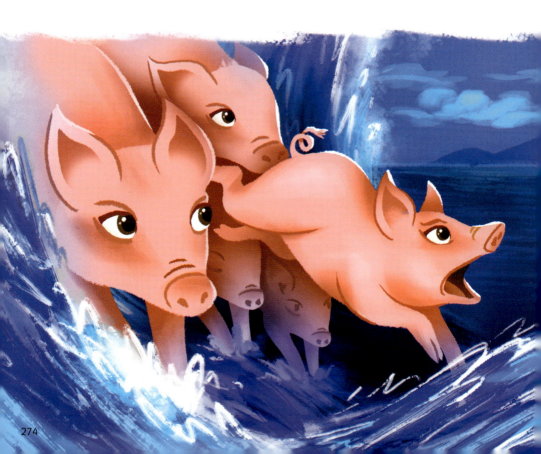

The man was completely changed. He was not mixed up anymore. "Go and tell everyone what has happened and what God has done for you," Jesus told him.

So he did!

61. Jesus Raises a Dead Girl to Life

Mark 5:21-42

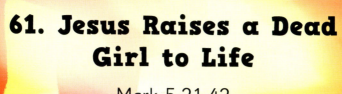

Jairus was an important leader of God's people. He had a 12-year-old daughter who was very, very sick.

So he went to find Jesus. "My daughter is dying," Jairus told him. "Please come and put your hands on her, so that she will get better and live."

Jesus started to walk to Jairus' house – but while he was on the way, some people brought Jairus some very sad news. "Your daughter has died," they told him. "There is nothing Jesus can do now."

"Don't be afraid," said Jesus. "Just believe in me."

When Jesus got to Jairus' house, lots of people were there. They were all crying because Jairus' daughter was dead.

"Why are you crying?" Jesus asked them.
"This girl is only asleep."

Everyone laughed at him. They knew she was not just asleep. She was not breathing. She was definitely dead.

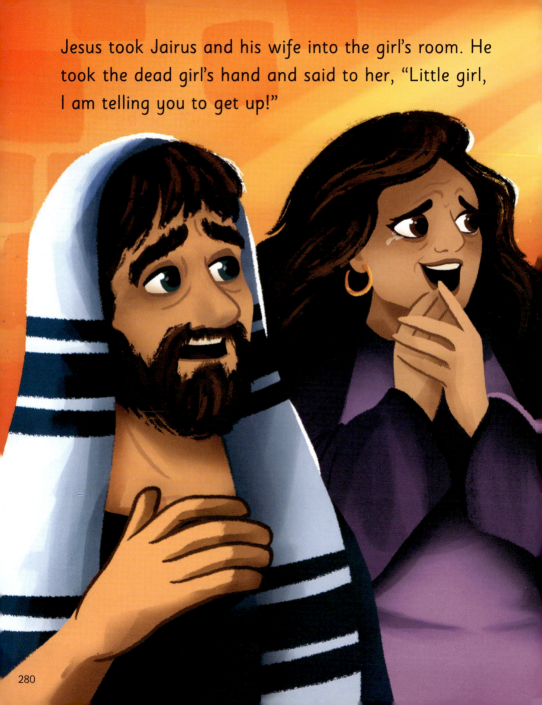
Jesus took Jairus and his wife into the girl's room. He took the dead girl's hand and said to her, "Little girl, I am telling you to get up!"

And she did! Jesus had raised her from being dead as easily as her father could wake her from being asleep. Her parents were completely amazed!

62. Buried Treasure

Matthew 13:44-46

Jesus used lots of stories to explain truths about who he is and how great it is to live as part of his kingdom with him as king. These stories were called parables.

Once, Jesus wanted to help his disciples understand that being part of his kingdom is more special than anything else in the whole world. So he told them two parables.

"My kingdom is like treasure that is buried in a field," Jesus told them. "When a man found the treasure, he went and sold everything he had so that he could buy the field and enjoy the treasure. He was so happy!

"My kingdom is also like someone looking for expensive pearls. When they find one which is really, really precious, they go and sell everything they have so they can buy it."

63. Jesus Feeds the Crowds

John 6:2-40

Lots and lots and lots of people had come to listen to Jesus. They were a long way from any towns, and they were getting hungry.

"Where could we buy bread for all these people to eat?" Jesus asked his friends.

"I would have to work for half a year to earn enough money to buy that much bread!" answered Philip.

Then Andrew said, "I have found a boy who has five small loaves of bread and two fish. But that will not feed all these people – not even close!"

Jesus told everyone to sit down. There were five thousand men, plus all the women and all the children.

Jesus took the loaves and fish and gave them to the disciples to give to the thousands of people. And he made it so that five loaves of bread and two fish became enough for everyone. Even once everyone was full, there were still twelve baskets of bread!

The next day, the people came back to see Jesus. They wanted more food!

"You need more than the normal bread I gave you yesterday," Jesus told them. "If you eat normal bread, it will give you life today. But I am the bread of life. If you believe in me, I will give you life with God forever."

64. Who Do You Say I Am?

Matthew 16:13-23

One day Jesus asked his disciples a question: "Who do people think I am?"

"Some people say you are John the Baptist," they answered. "But some people think you are God's messenger Elijah. And some people think that you are one of God's other messengers from long ago."

"What about you?" Jesus asked his friends. "Who do *you* say I am?"

"You are God's chosen, promise-keeping king – the king we need. You are the Son of God," answered Peter.

Jesus then started to explain what would happen to him. "Lots of painful things are going to be done to me," he told them. "The leaders will not like me. I will be killed. But then, three days later, I will rise back to life."

Peter was not happy about what Jesus had said. "That must never happen to you!" he said.

Jesus was *really* not happy with what Peter had said! "You are wrong," he said. "You need to stop thinking about your own ideas about me and start listening to God's special plan for me."

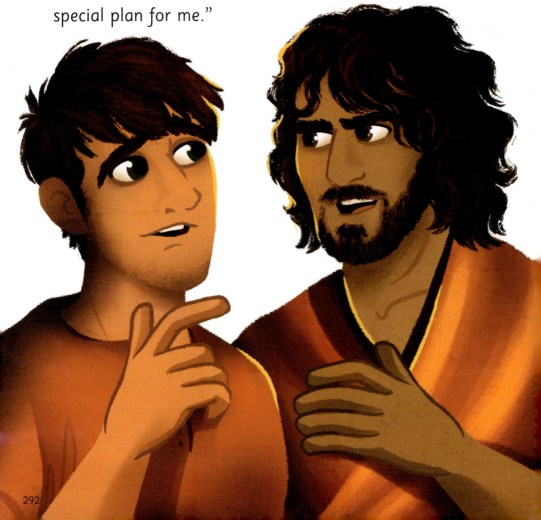

65. Jesus on the Mountain

Matthew 17:1-9; Mark 9:2-10

Jesus took his friends Peter, James, and John up a mountain to pray. While he was praying, the way that Jesus looked became very different — his face shone like the sun, and his clothes became as bright as lightning.

Two of God's messengers from hundreds of years before, Moses and Elijah, came from heaven to talk with him.

The disciples were very scared. They did not know what to say or what to do!

Then God spoke from a cloud. "This is my Son," God said. "I love him. I am very pleased with him. Listen to him!"

The disciples were so frightened that they fell over. Jesus helped them get up. "Don't be afraid," he said. When they looked around, the cloud had gone and they could not see Moses or Elijah.

As they walked back down the mountain, Jesus told his friends not to tell anyone what they had seen until after he had risen from the dead. "Risen from the dead?" they said to each other. "What does he mean?"

66. The Good Samaritan

Luke 10:25-37

Jesus told a story to help people understand how to love others. His story was about three men from Judah and one man from Samaria. (People from Judah and Samaria did not like each other at all.)

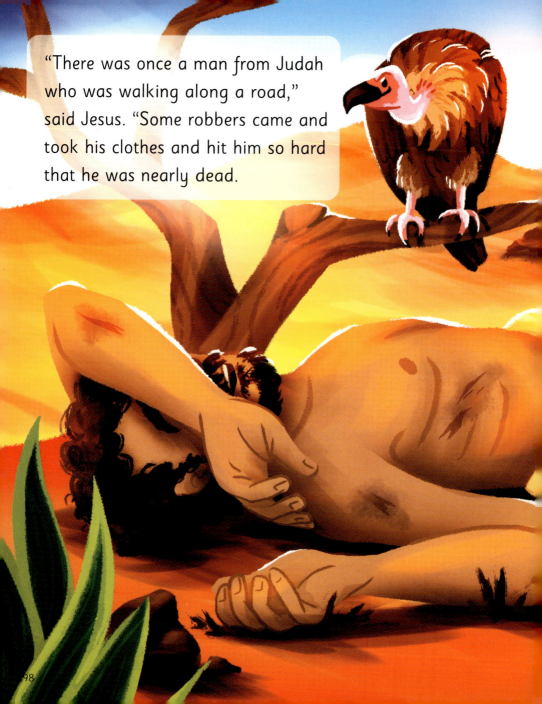

"There was once a man from Judah who was walking along a road," said Jesus. "Some robbers came and took his clothes and hit him so hard that he was nearly dead.

"A religious man from Judah came along that road. He saw the badly hurt man — but he just walked past him. Then another religious man from Judah came along the road — but he just walked past the badly hurt man too.

"Then a Samaritan man came along the road. He saw the badly hurt man from Judah. He stopped... he helped him... he took him to a place where he could care for him... and then he paid someone to keep caring for the man."

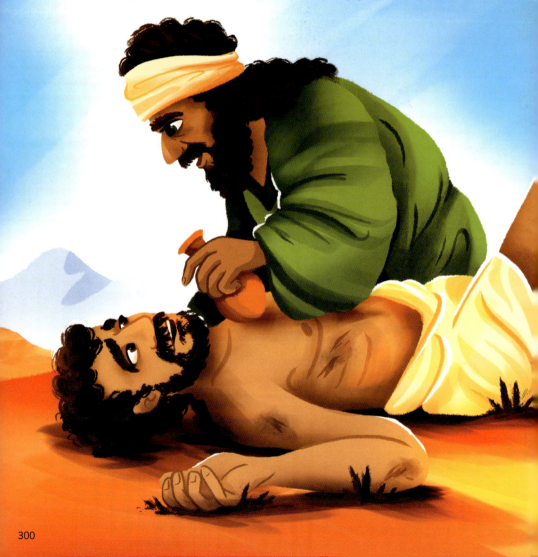

Then Jesus asked, "Which of those men was truly loving others? You go and be kind like him. People who truly love God will show it by truly loving others."

67. Jesus Teaches His Friends to Pray

Matthew 6:9-13; Luke 11:1-13

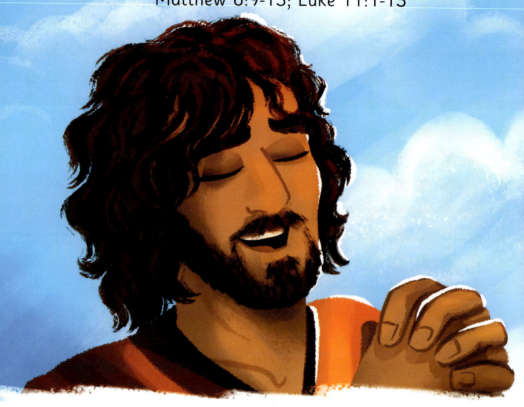

Jesus was praying. When he finished, one of his disciples asked him, "Please teach us to pray."

Jesus answered, "When you pray, say:

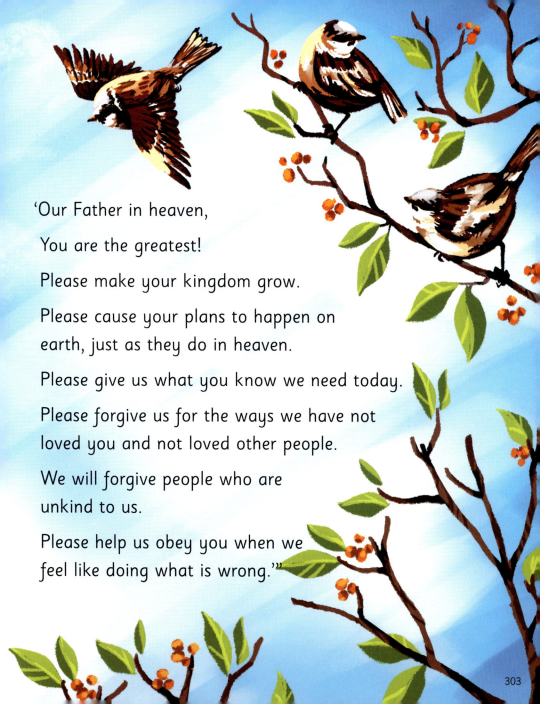

'Our Father in heaven,

You are the greatest!

Please make your kingdom grow.

Please cause your plans to happen on earth, just as they do in heaven.

Please give us what you know we need today.

Please forgive us for the ways we have not loved you and not loved other people.

We will forgive people who are unkind to us.

Please help us obey you when we feel like doing what is wrong.'"

Then Jesus said, "If a child asks their daddy for a fish to eat, he would never give them a snake instead! Daddies should give good things to their children. Well, because you live with me as your king, God is your Father in heaven. He is even better at giving good gifts to his children than daddies on earth are. He will even give you his Holy Spirit!"

68. The Good Shepherd

Luke 15:3-7; John 10:1-15

Jesus told a story to show how much God loves his people:

"A shepherd had a hundred sheep. But one of them got lost. So the shepherd left the rest of his sheep and went looking for his lost one.

"He searched and searched until... he found it! He was so happy!

"He put the sheep on his shoulders and took it home. Then the shepherd called his friends and said, 'I have found my lost sheep! Come and have a party with me!'

"Sometimes, someone who has not been loving God or trying to obey God admits that they have been living in the wrong way. So they start living with God in charge and they ask God to forgive them. Whenever someone does that, God has a party in heaven."

Another time, Jesus said to his friends, "I am like a shepherd and my people are like my sheep. My sheep listen to my voice and obey me. I care for my sheep and I lead my sheep. I love my sheep so much that I will even die to make them safe. I am the good shepherd."

69. The Life After This One

Luke 16:19-31

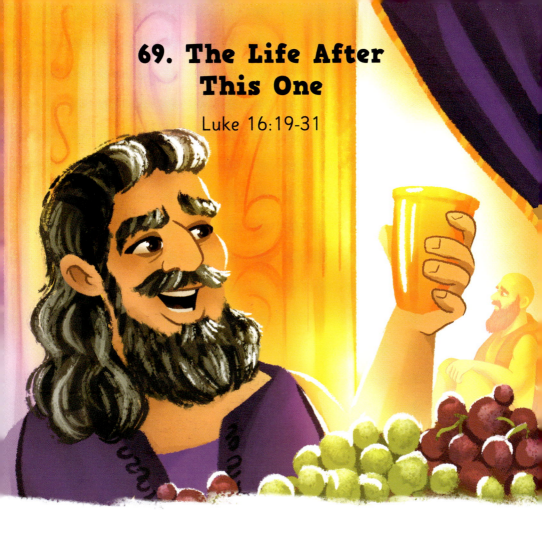

Jesus told a story to show that what happens after we die matters more than what happens in this life:

"Once there were two men. One was rich. He had expensive clothes, ate yummy food, and had everything he wanted.

"The other man was called Lazarus. He was poor. He had no food and no home. Lazarus sat outside the rich man's door, hoping someone would give him something to eat.

"One day Lazarus died, and God took him to live with him in the life after this one.

"Then the rich man died. He hadn't listened to God's messengers telling him to love and obey God and to ask him for forgiveness – and so he was not able to be where Lazarus was. Instead, he went to a place where there was nothing good. He was filled up with deep sadness.

"The rich man asked if Lazarus could help. But there was a great gap between them, and no one could cross it, ever.

"So the rich man asked if someone could tell his brothers about the life after this one," Jesus said. "But of course they already had people to tell them about it. They had God's messengers they could listen to – especially the messenger who would rise from the dead."

70. The Religious Leader and the Tax Collector

Luke 18:9-14

Some people thought that they were really good people and so God would definitely want them to live with him in his kingdom forever. So Jesus told them this story:

"Two men went to the temple to pray. One of them was a religious leader who took God's rules very seriously. Everyone thought he was a very good person.

"The religious leader prayed, 'God, thank you that I am a better person than people like this tax collector. I am good at obeying you.'

"The other man was a tax collector who had broken lots of God's rules. Everyone thought he was a very bad person.

"The tax collector prayed in a sad voice, 'God, I know I am not a good person. I have not obeyed you. Please forgive me.'

"The tax collector went home as God's forgiven friend, but the religious leader did not," said Jesus.

"Some people think they are good enough to be friends with God. But they will find out one day that they are not God's friends at all. Some people know they are not good enough, and they ask God to forgive them. Those people are friends with God."

71. Jesus and the Little Children

Mark 10:13-16

Some little children and their parents came to see Jesus. The children wanted to be friends with him.

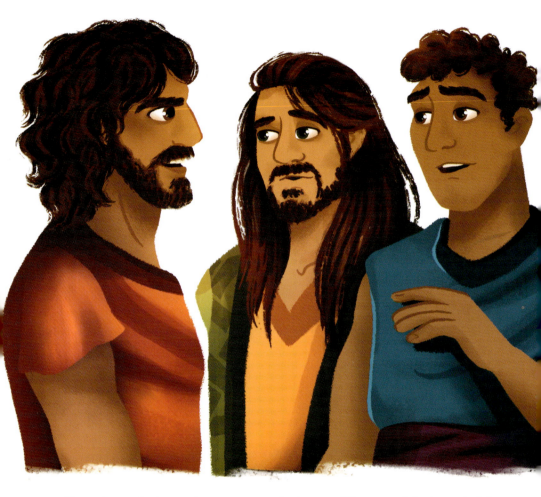

But Jesus' disciples stopped them. They told the children they were wrong to think that Jesus would want to spend time with them.

When Jesus saw this, he was very unhappy with the disciples.

"Let the children come to me," he told them. "My kingdom belongs to people like them. To be part of my kingdom, you all need to be like a little child — you all just need to come and ask me to be your friend and your king."

Then Jesus welcomed the little children and they came and sat on his knee. He told them that they were his friends, who could enjoy living under his rule and being happy in his world.

72. Zacchaeus Welcomes Jesus

Luke 19:1-10

Zacchaeus was a tax collector. He was rich because he took money from other people and kept lots of it for himself.

One day, Zacchaeus heard that Jesus was in his town. He wanted to see Jesus — but he was a small man and he could not see over everyone else's heads. So he climbed a tree to get a better view.

When Jesus reached Zacchaeus' tree, he stopped. "Zacchaeus," he said, "I would like to stay at your house today."

Zacchaeus scrambled down his tree. He felt really happy that Jesus wanted to spend time with him.

Everyone else felt very *not* happy. "Why is Jesus choosing to spend time with a mean cheater instead of good people?" they grumbled.

But Zacchaeus had changed. "Jesus, I am going to give half of my money to people who have less than me," he said. "And I will give back everything I have stolen, plus extra."

Jesus said, "Today you have been rescued. I came to find and rescue lost people like you."

73. The King on the Donkey

Matthew 21:1-9; Luke 19:28-40

Hundreds of years before Jesus was born, God's messenger Zechariah had said that when God's promise-keeping king came, he would ride into Jerusalem on a young donkey.

Jesus and his friends were near Jerusalem. So he sent two of his disciples to a village. "You will find a young donkey there," he told them. "Untie it and bring it to me."

The disciples found the donkey just as Jesus had said they would, and Jesus rode it into Jerusalem. Crowds of people spread their cloaks and tree branches across the road in front of him.

"Yay, this is the king from great King David's family! This is the king God promised to send!" they shouted. "This is the king who will bring happiness because he has come from God!"

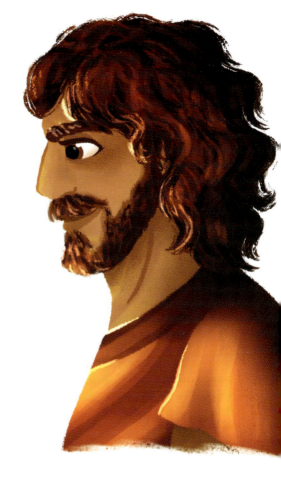

Some of the religious leaders were not happy, though. "Tell these people to stop saying these things about you," they grumbled to Jesus.

Jesus said, "If these people have to keep quiet, I will get the stones on this road to shout about who I am." And off he rode, on his donkey, into Jerusalem.

74. Jesus at the Temple
Matthew 21:12-16

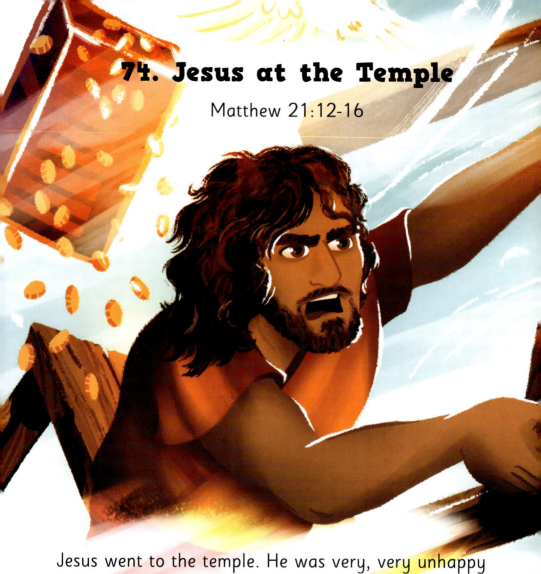

Jesus went to the temple. He was very, very unhappy about what he saw there, because people were using it as a shop where they could make money instead of as a place where they could pray to God.

So Jesus tipped over the tables of the people who were selling things. "God has said this should be a place for people from all over the world to pray in," he said. "But you are using it to steal from others."

The religious leaders were angry. They wanted to get rid of Jesus. Then they heard some children shouting, "Jesus is the king from great King David's family. Yay!" Now they were even more angry.

"Do you hear those children, Jesus?" they complained. "They are saying you are God's promise-keeping king."

"Yes, they are," answered Jesus. "God loves to hear big truths coming out of little mouths."

75. A New Special Meal

Matthew 26:26-29; Luke 22:37;
John 14:6

It was one of the most special days of the year – the day to remember how, long ago, God had rescued the Israelites from Egypt and made an unbreakable promise to love them as his people. Jesus and his friends shared the special remembering meal.

Jesus knew that soon he would die on a cross. He wanted his friends to understand why he would let that happen. So he took some bread and broke it into pieces. "Whenever you eat bread together, I would like you to remember that my body was broken to rescue you," Jesus said.

Then Jesus took a cup of wine. "Whenever you drink wine together, remember that I bled on the cross so that you can be forgiven," he said. "I am making a new unbreakable promise to you. You will always be God's forgiven people.

"It is time for me to keep all the promises God has made," Jesus told his disciples. "It is time for me to take the punishment you deserve for not loving and obeying God.

"I am the way to God's place.

"I tell the truth about God's place.

"I give people life in God's place."

76. Praying in a Garden

Luke 22:39-46; Mark 14:32-41

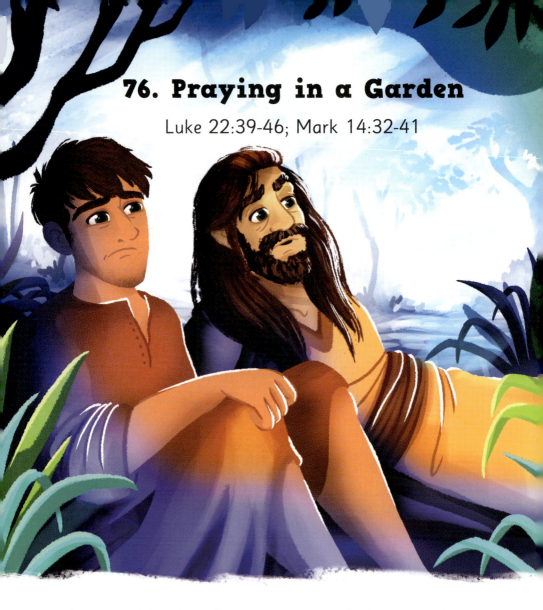

Jesus and his friends went to a garden to pray. It was very late and everyone was really tired.

Jesus was feeling very, very sad. He knew that soon it would be time for him to die, and he knew that that would be very, very hard. So he spoke to his Father:

"Dear Father, you can do anything. I would like you to take away the awful things that are going to happen to me. But most of all, I would like to do what you want me to do."

The disciples were so tired that instead of helping Jesus, they fell asleep while he prayed. But God sent an angel to help Jesus and give him strength.

Jesus woke his friends up. "It is time," he told them. "God's promises are coming true now."

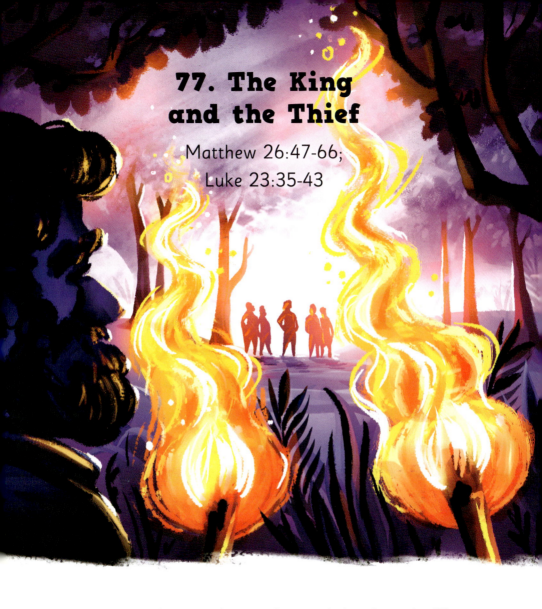

77. The King and the Thief

Matthew 26:47-66;
Luke 23:35-43

Jesus was standing in the garden with his friends. The religious leaders came with soldiers to take him away.

"Tell us the truth," the leaders demanded. "Are you really God's chosen king? Are you really the Son of God?"

"Yes," answered Jesus. "And one day you will see me sitting on a throne and ruling over everything forever."

"We do not believe you!" said the religious leaders. "It is time to get rid of you!"

They took Jesus outside the city and put him on a cross. "You don't look like a rescuing king now!" they shouted.

A thief was put on a cross next to Jesus. He said...

"Jesus, I know I deserve to be punished for what I have done wrong.

"Jesus, I know that you don't deserve to be punished, because you have never done anything wrong.

"Jesus, I know you are the king. Please could I have a place in your kingdom in the life after this one?"

Jesus answered him, "I promise that today, after we have both died, you will be with me in my wonderful place."

Then Jesus died. A soldier who was watching said, "This man really was the Son of God!"

78. Jesus Is Alive!

Matthew 27:60 – 28:10;
Luke 24:1-9

Jesus died on a Friday. His friends put him in a tomb, and a huge, heavy stone was rolled across its entrance. They felt very, very sad — sadder than they had ever felt before.

On the Saturday everyone rested. On the Sunday some of Jesus' friends, called Mary, Mary, and Salome, went to his tomb...

Jesus was not there.

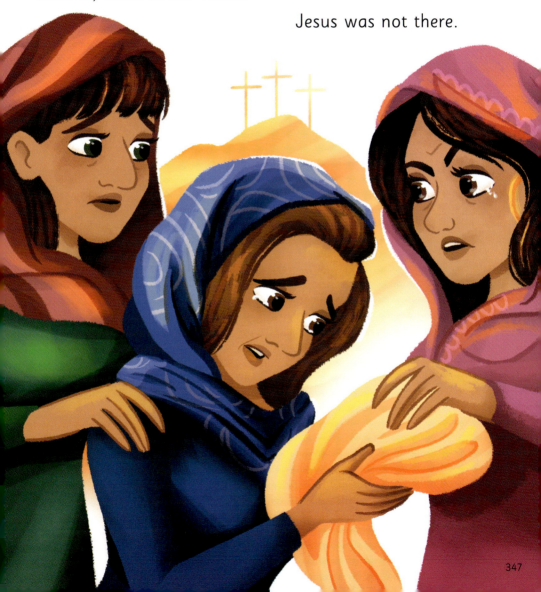

Suddenly two angels appeared. The women were terrified!

"Don't be afraid," the angels said. "Jesus is not here because Jesus is alive! He promised you that he would be killed and then rise back to life. And he's kept his promise!"

The women were still a bit frightened, but now they were mainly filled up with happiness. Then suddenly Jesus himself stood in front of them. "Hello!" he greeted the women. "Go and tell my friends that soon they will get to see me!"

79. The Strange Stranger
Luke 24:13-35

It was Sunday afternoon, and two of Jesus' friends were walking from Jerusalem to a village called Emmaus. They were full of sadness because they had thought that Jesus was God's promise-keeping king – but then he had died.

As they walked along, a stranger came and walked with them. Jesus' friends told him why they were so sad.

"You don't seem to believe what God's messengers promised," the strange stranger replied. "Hundreds of years ago, God's messengers said that God's promise-keeping king would die. But remember that those messengers also said that after he had died, God's king would rule forever."

When they got to Emmaus it was getting late, so Jesus' friends invited the strange stranger to have a meal with them. He took some bread and broke it into pieces... and at that exact moment God allowed the men to see that this stranger was not a stranger at all! It was Jesus!

Jesus disappeared. So the men rushed back to Jerusalem to tell Jesus' other friends that he was alive. While they were talking, Jesus appeared again and ate some fish. "I am making all God's promises come true," Jesus told them.

80. Thomas Changes His Mind

John 20:24-29

Thomas was one of Jesus' friends, but he had not been there when the other disciples had seen Jesus.

"We have seen King Jesus alive!" all the others told Thomas.

"I don't believe it," replied Thomas. "Jesus died on a cross. Unless I see him and touch him, I will not believe that Jesus is alive."

For a whole week, Thomas carried on not believing that Jesus was alive.

Then, when the disciples were meeting together in a house with locked doors, suddenly Jesus was there!

Jesus said to Thomas, "Look at my hands, which were fixed to the cross. Touch me. Believe that I am alive."

Thomas replied, "You are my king and my God."

Jesus said, "Thomas, because you have seen me, you believe that I am alive. Now you are blessed – you can live under my rule and be happy in my world.

"Lots of other people who don't get to see me will also believe that I am alive. Then they will also enjoy living under my rule and being happy in my world."

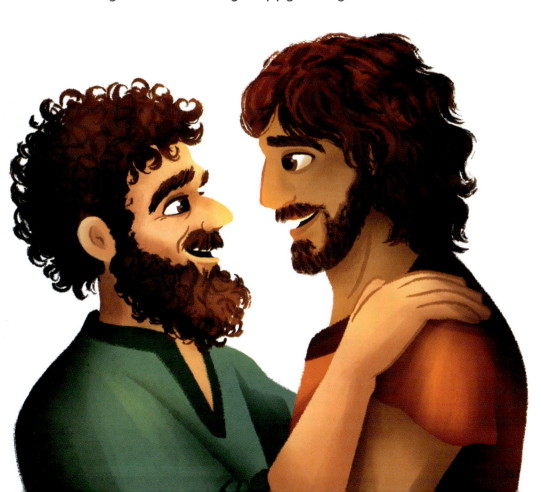

81. Jesus Goes to Heaven

Luke 24:46-49; Acts 1:4-11

It was time for Jesus to go back to heaven to be with his Father.

"I am going to give you a gift," he told his friends. "I will pour the Holy Spirit into all of you.

"And I am giving you a job," continued Jesus. "I want you to tell people the truth about who I am, and that anyone can live with me as their king and be forgiven.

"I want you to tell people in this city about me, and then people in this country about me, and then people in the countries near here about me, and then people throughout the whole world about me!

"You will need help to do this – and the Holy Spirit will give you everything you need."

Then Jesus left his friends and went to heaven. He disappeared behind a cloud. They couldn't see him anymore.

Suddenly two angels were standing next to them. "Today, Jesus has gone back to heaven," they said. "One day, he will come back to earth."

82. The Holy Spirit Arrives

Acts 2:1-41

Jesus' friends were in a house in Jerusalem when they heard a whooshing sound like a mighty wind. Then they saw a fire that wasn't burning anything. It split into smaller fires that came to sit on each of them. It was God's Holy Spirit!

Straightaway all the disciples were able to speak in different languages.

There was a festival happening that day called Pentecost. People from all over the world were there. They heard the disciples talking about God in all their different languages.

"What is going on?!" they asked.

Peter told them: "Long ago, God sent a messenger called Joel to promise that one day God would pour his Spirit into all his people. You have seen that promise come true."

Then Peter told them about Jesus: "Jesus did many great things. God's plan was for him to die and then rise back to life – and he did. We saw it! Jesus is the promise-keeping king. You need to live with him as *your* king and ask him to forgive *you* – and then he will pour his Spirit into you too."

Anyone who wanted to start living with Jesus as their king was baptized. On that one day, three thousand people became friends with Jesus.

83. The First Church

Acts 2:42-47

Jesus' friends loved listening to the disciples' teaching about Jesus. They loved meeting together. They loved eating bread together and remembering that Jesus' body had been broken on the cross to rescue them. They loved praying together.

Because Jesus' friends loved each other, they shared their things so that everyone had enough. They sold some of their things so that they could give money to people who didn't have any.

Each day they would meet together near the temple in Jerusalem and sing praises to Jesus. The Holy Spirit gave the disciples power to do amazing things.

Everyone in Jerusalem heard about what was going on. The meetings got bigger and bigger as more and more people decided they wanted to live with Jesus as their king too.

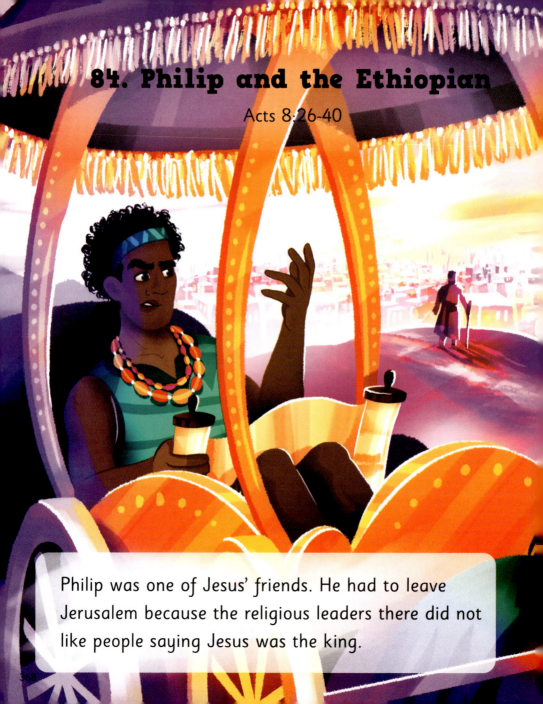

84. Philip and the Ethiopian
Acts 8:26-40

Philip was one of Jesus' friends. He had to leave Jerusalem because the religious leaders there did not like people saying Jesus was the king.

One day an angel told Philip to walk along a particular road – so he did. There he saw a chariot. The man sitting in it was a very important person from a faraway country called Ethiopia. He was reading the words of God's messenger Isaiah, about someone who would die like a lamb even though he did not deserve to be punished.

God's Holy Spirit told Philip to go and talk to the Ethiopian — so he did.

"Do you understand what you are reading?" Philip asked him.

"No," said the man. "I am full of confusion about who Isaiah was talking about. Do you know?"

Philip did know! He told the Ethiopian that Isaiah was talking about Jesus. He explained that Jesus was God's promise-keeping king who had died to rescue his people.

The Ethiopian wanted to live with Jesus as his king. He asked Philip to baptize him to show he was part of God's people. Then the Ethiopian carried on home. Now he wasn't full of confusion — now he was full of happiness.

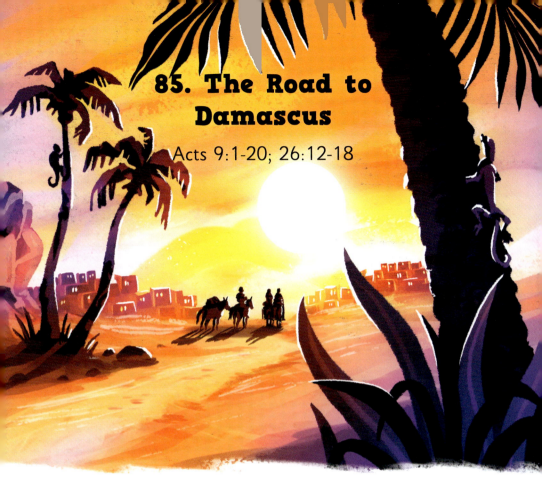

85. The Road to Damascus

Acts 9:1-20; 26:12-18

In Jerusalem lived a man named Paul who REALLY did not like Jesus and his friends. He wanted to stop anyone talking about Jesus.

One day Paul was on his way to the city of Damascus. His plan was to put all Jesus' friends there in prison.

But as Paul walked along the road, suddenly a light brighter than the sun flashed around him. He fell to the ground. And a voice spoke: "Paul, Paul, why are you trying to harm me by hurting my friends?"

"Who are you?" said Paul.

"I am Jesus," answered the voice. "I have chosen you to go and tell people all over the world about me. Now get up, go into Damascus, and wait."

When Paul got up, he couldn't see. He went to Damascus and waited.

In Damascus lived a friend of Jesus called Ananias. Jesus spoke to him in a vision: "Go and find Paul. Put your hand on him and I will make him see again."

Ananias was very surprised but he obeyed Jesus. Paul's eyes started working again, and he was baptized. Then the man who had wanted to stop anyone talking about Jesus started talking to everyone about Jesus!

86. The One Who Keeps God's Promises

Acts 13:13 – 14:1

Paul and his friend Barnabas went to the city of Antioch to tell people there about Jesus.

"Long, long ago, God promised Abraham a huge family," they said. "God promised to give Abraham's family a land to live in, and he promised to use Abraham's family to bless people who lived all over the world.

"He promised to give them a king who would rescue his people. And God made lots and lots more promises through the years.

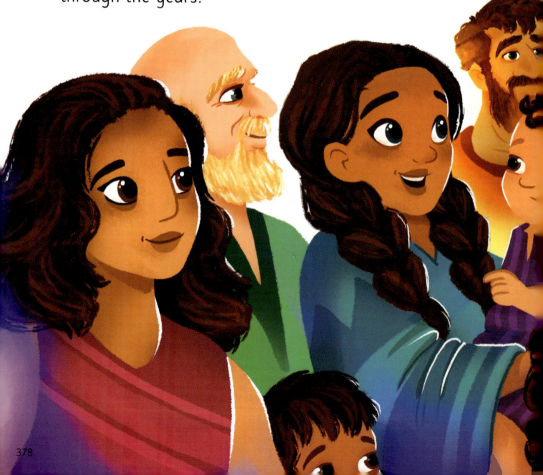

"We are here to tell you about Jesus. He is the rescuer God promised to send. He died, but then he rose back to life. He is the one who keeps all of God's unbreakable promises."

Some people believed their message, and so the number of people living with Jesus as king got bigger and bigger. But at the same time, some people did not like the message, and they got angrier and angrier. They made Paul and Barnabas leave Antioch – so they went to the nearby city of Iconium and told people there about Jesus instead!

87. Jesus' Friends in Philippi

Acts 16:11-34

In Philippi, a city in Greece, Paul and his friend Silas met a woman called Lydia. When Paul told her his message, God made her able to believe in Jesus. "Please stay at my house while you're here," she said.

Next, Paul and Silas were walking down the road when they saw a girl who was a slave. An evil spirit had made her life go very wrong. Paul said to the evil spirit, "I am speaking to you with King Jesus' power. Come out of her."

And it did.

The men who had been making the girl work for them were angry about what had happened, and they put Paul and Silas in prison. But in the middle of the night, while Paul and Silas were singing songs about Jesus, there was an earthquake, and all the prison doors swung open.

The prison guard knew he needed to listen to Paul and Silas' message. "What must I do to be rescued by God?" he asked.

"Believe in Jesus as your king, and you will be rescued," said Paul and Silas.

So he did, and so did his whole family. They were baptized, they ate with Paul and Silas, and they were filled with happiness.

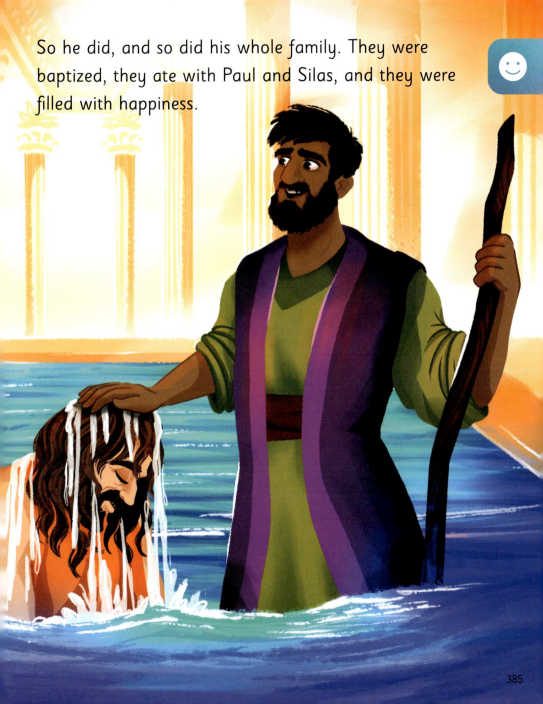

88. Paul in Jerusalem and Rome

Acts 21 – 28

When Jesus' friends told others about him, some people were really happy, and they became friends with Jesus too. But some people were really annoyed, and they tried to keep Jesus' friends quiet.

Once, when Paul was in Jerusalem telling people about Jesus, soldiers put him in prison. Paul had to go and see the most powerful person in the country — the Roman governor. He could decide whether Paul would go free or stay in prison — or even die. Paul told the governor about Jesus.

After a while there was a new governor, so Paul told him about Jesus too. This governor asked a king who lived nearby to ask Paul some questions. So Paul told him about Jesus too.

Eventually, Paul was put on a boat to go to Rome to see the emperor. Rome was the most important city in the world. On the boat, Paul told the sailors about Jesus.

When Paul reached Rome he was put in a house and not allowed to leave. So he invited lots of people to come and see him and... he told them about Jesus as well!

(We don't know what happened when Paul went to see the emperor. But you can probably guess.)

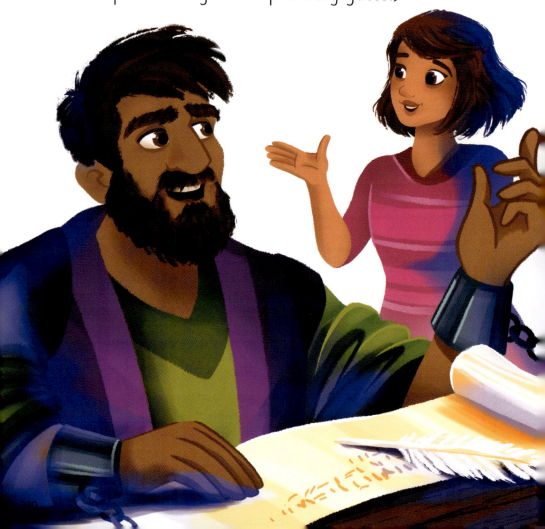

89. Paul's Letters

When people decided to live with Jesus as their king, they started meeting together. These groups were called churches.

Paul wrote letters to the churches. The letters reminded them about how much Jesus loved them and taught them how to obey him. Paul answered their questions and helped them with any problems they had.

Two of Paul's letters were to the church in Corinth. One thing Paul explained to them is that a church is like a body. Just like a body needs its eyes and fingers and toes to work together, a church needs everyone who is part of it to work together and take care of each other.

Another of Paul's letters was to the churches in Galatia. He reminded them that they only needed to do one thing to enjoy being with God in the life after this one. That one thing, he told them, wasn't to be really good at obeying Jesus — it was to believe that they were forgiven by Jesus.

Paul also wrote letters to his friends, like Timothy, Titus, and Philemon. He encouraged them to keep loving their churches and to keep telling other people about King Jesus.

90. More Letters

Just like Paul wrote letters to churches, so did some of Jesus' other friends.

One of them wrote the letter to the Hebrews. His main message was "Jesus is the best, and believing God's promises is great."

James was Jesus' brother. He wrote a letter to some churches to tell them, "We show we are friends with Jesus by trying to obey Jesus. And when you don't obey him, remember God is always kind to people who are sorry."

Jesus' disciple Peter wrote two letters, and another man called Jude also wrote a letter. Their message was "When life is hard, make sure you keep believing the truth about Jesus, whatever anyone says. Being friends with Jesus means we always have lots of reasons to be happy."

Jesus' disciple John wrote three letters to churches. Their main message was "If Jesus is your king, then God really, really, really, really, really loves you, because you are his children."

91. What Heaven Is Like

Revelation 1:9-19; 5:1-14; 7:9-17

When Jesus' friend John was very old, King Jesus showed him what heaven was like. Jesus' hair was white like snow, and his eyes were blazing like fire. His feet were like glowing bronze, and his face was shining like the sun.

John saw that in the middle of heaven Jesus was sitting on his throne, ruling over everything forever. The throne had a rainbow going round it, and around the throne were lots and lots and lots of people. There were so many of them that they were as hard to count as the stars in the sky or as the dust in the world. They spoke every language there was, and they came from every country.

All these people were singing, "We love praising you, God, because you made everything. We love praising you, Jesus, because you died to rescue us so that we can enjoy this place with you forever."

Then thousands and thousands and thousands of angels joined in. And so did millions of animals and sea creatures.

"Tell all my friends what you have seen," Jesus told John. "I know that it is often hard to live with me as king. Tell them that one day they will be with me in the life after this one."

92. I Am Coming Soon

Revelation 20:2, 10; 21 – 22

Jesus also showed John what will happen in the future, on a day that has not yet come.

John saw a snake. The snake was the devil. He saw Jesus get rid of the devil so that the devil could not make anything go wrong ever again.

John saw Jesus come back to earth and put everything right again. All the people who loved Jesus as their king were living there with him. John saw that no one was ever sad and no one ever needed to cry.

John saw that the world looked a little bit like the city of Jerusalem and a little bit like the garden God had made in the beginning. He saw God's throne, and he saw God's Special Tree, which people could eat from to stay alive. Everyone could eat from it every day, and never die.

Everything was perfect, and everyone was perfect. Everyone enjoyed living under Jesus' rule and everyone was happy in Jesus' perfect world. All God's promises had come true.

"Tell all my friends that I promise that these things will definitely happen," Jesus said to John.

"I am coming soon."

WHAT NEXT?

The Bible is **ONE BIG TRUE STORY** — and you can be a part of that story too! Because God sent his Son Jesus to keep all his promises, anyone who becomes Jesus' friend can enjoy life with him forever in his perfect world in the life after this one.

When Jesus lived in this world, he told people, "Because I have arrived, people can be part of God's kingdom. You need to love and obey me as your King and believe that I make all God's promises come true" (Mark 1:15, my paraphrase).

You could talk to him now, if you like! You could say:

> "Jesus, you are the King. You make all God's promises come true. I love you. I want to obey you. Please give me a place in your kingdom in the life after this one."

And do you know what Jesus replies to anyone who says this to him? He says the same as he said to the thief who was hanging on a cross next to him as he died:

"I promise that you will be with me in my wonderful place" (Luke 23:43, my paraphrase).

And, as we have seen, God always keeps his promises!

GOD'S BIG PROMISES
Family Resources

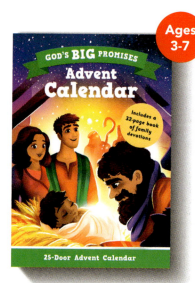

Ages 3-7

Advent Calendar and Family Devotions

This attractive 25-door Advent calendar for children aged 3-7 years old is linked with *God's Big Promises Bible Storybook*. It also comes with a booklet containing 25 short, simple devotions for December, to help families explore the Christmas story together.

✓ thegoodbook.com | co.uk

Bible Heroes Sticker and Activity Book

Using vibrant illustrations and simple, faithful teaching from *God's Big Promises Bible Storybook*, this sticker and activity book features 16 pages of puzzles and games and over 60 stickers based on the heroes of the Bible story, all of whom point to Jesus, the greatest hero of all. Perfect for kids aged 3-7.

Christmas Sticker and Activity Book

Brings the Christmas story to life with 16 pages of puzzles and games and over 60 stickers! Based on *God's Big Promises Bible Storybook*.

See all related resources and download freebies at
godsbigpromises.com

Easter Sticker and Activity Book

Using vibrant illustrations and simple, faithful teaching from *God's Big Promises Bible Storybook*, this activity book helps kids engage with the Easter story. It features over 60 stickers and 16 pages of puzzles, games, and other activities.

Easter for Little Ones

Using simple sentences and stunning illustrations from *God's Big Promises Bible Storybook*, this board book takes toddlers aged 1-3 through the story of the first Easter, showing what happened and that King Jesus is alive again.

See all related resources and download freebies at

godsbigpromises.com

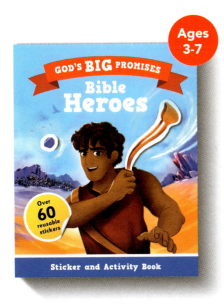

Bible Heroes Sticker and Activity Book

Using vibrant illustrations and simple, faithful teaching from *God's Big Promises Bible Storybook*, this sticker and activity book features 16 pages of puzzles and games and over 60 stickers based on the heroes of the Bible story, all of whom point to Jesus, the greatest hero of all. Perfect for kids aged 3-7.

Christmas Sticker and Activity Book

Brings the Christmas story to life with 16 pages of puzzles and games and over 60 stickers! Based on *God's Big Promises Bible Storybook*.

See all related resources and download freebies at
godsbigpromises.com

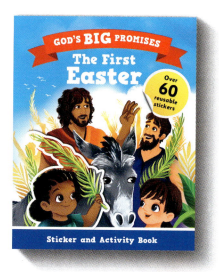

Easter Sticker and Activity Book

Using vibrant illustrations and simple, faithful teaching from *God's Big Promises Bible Storybook*, this activity book helps kids engage with the Easter story. It features over 60 stickers and 16 pages of puzzles, games, and other activities.

Easter for Little Ones

Using simple sentences and stunning illustrations from *God's Big Promises Bible Storybook*, this board book takes toddlers aged 1-3 through the story of the first Easter, showing what happened and that King Jesus is alive again.

See all related resources and download freebies at

Also by Carl Laferton

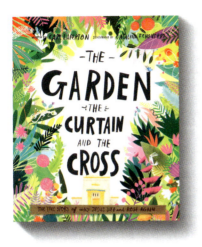

This best-selling 32-page storybook takes children on a journey from the Garden of Eden to God's perfect new creation. Kids aged 3-6 will learn why Jesus died and rose again, and why it's the best news ever.

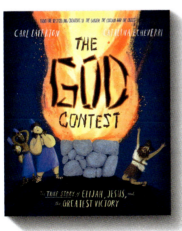

This award-winning book tells the gripping story of how the God of the Bible proved himself to be the one true God in the time of Elijah—and how he did so again, supremely, by raising Jesus from the dead.

 thegoodbook.com | co.uk

BIBLICAL | RELEVANT | ACCESSIBLE

At The Good Book Company, we are dedicated to helping Christians and local churches grow. We believe that God's growth process always starts with hearing clearly what he has said to us through his timeless word—the Bible.

Ever since we opened our doors in 1991, we have been striving to produce Bible-based resources that bring glory to God. We have grown to become an international provider of user-friendly resources to the Christian community, with believers of all backgrounds and denominations using our books, Bible studies, devotionals, evangelistic resources, and DVD-based courses.

We want to equip ordinary Christians to live for Christ day by day, and churches to grow in their knowledge of God, their love for one another, and the effectiveness of their outreach.

Call us for a discussion of your needs or visit one of our local websites for more information on the resources and services we provide.

Your friends at The Good Book Company

thegoodbook.com | thegoodbook.co.uk
thegoodbook.com.au | thegoodbook.co.nz
thegoodbook.co.in